Lighthouse Secrets

A Collection of Recipes from
the Nation's Oldest City

THE JUNIOR SERVICE LEAGUE
OF ST. AUGUSTINE, INC.

Lighthouse
Secrets

The Junior Service League of St. Augustine is a non-profit organization founded in 1935 to address civic, social, cultural and service needs of St. John's County. In its 64 years of existence, the Junior Service League has been a force for positive change, as well as a source of volunteer leadership and funding for many important causes in our community. The League's most recent project was the restoration of the historic St. Augustine Light Station. After 15 years of dedicated effort, the final phase was finished in 1995. Since the completion of the Light Station project, the Junior Service League has been laying the groundwork for the first Family Visitation Center in St. Augustine, which we hope will open in 1999.

Proceeds from the sale of *Lighthouse Secrets* will be returned to the community through the League's support of these and other volunteer projects.

Additional copies of *Lighthouse Secrets* may be obtained by sending $19.95 plus $3.50 per book for shipping and handling to:

Lighthouse Secrets
Junior Service League of St. Augustine, Inc.
P.O. Box 374
St. Augustine, FL 32085

First Printing, April, 1999

Copyright ©1999

The Junior Service of St. Augustine, Inc.

All rights reserved

ISBN Number 0-9670320-0-8

Printed in the USA by

WIMMER
The Wimmer Companies
Memphis
1-800-548-2537

Committee

Lighthouse Secrets is the result of three years of dedication and effort on the part of the following committee members and their families:

Susan Partel
Chairman

Jane R. Masson
Chairman

Betty Crosby
Active Sustaining Chairman

Debbie Adams	Kim Lhota
Marilyn Beach	Bridget O'Connor-Carmichael
Debbie Burkhardt	Colette Parker
Sherri Cone	Elizabeth Schrum
Beverly Fowdy	Michelle Tasker
Rita George	Jennifer Tesori
Tammy Grimes	Cathy Upchurch
Sue Hale	Catalina Usina-Morse
Kristen Hébert	Stevie Weimer
Lee Livingston	Jane Wood

The Junior Service League wishes to thank these talented individuals who gave their time and energy to the professionalism of this book. We deeply appreciate you.

Pat Madden

Award winning Pat Madden paints in the bold warm colors that depict 400 plus years of Spanish history in St. Augustine, the Nation's Oldest City. His spectacular use of color enhances the beauty of the primary images within each subject. Extensive travel throughout Florida, Central America and the Caribbean has greatly influenced his style. These experiences, coupled with his formal art training at Florida School of the Arts and Palm Beach Junior College, sparked in him a passion for sharing his vision of St. Augustine through art. His work has been exhibited throughout the United States in regional and national exhibitions, as well as private and corporate collections. Madden currently resides in St. Augustine with his wife and two children.

David Nolan

Histories of the buildings and places depicted in this book were provided by David Nolan, author of Fifty Feet in Paradise: The Booming of Florida (1984) and The Houses of St. Augustine (1995). He is a longtime supporter of the Junior Service League in its efforts to preserve the historic lighthouse and lightkeepers house.

About St. Augustine

St. Augustine, America's Oldest City is a unique and wonderful combination of romantic, historical, dining and shopping experiences. The city that is steeped in nearly 500 years of history is also brimming with modern encounters that give this area a special blend that offers something for everyone. Founded in 1565, St. Augustine is the oldest continuously occupied European settlement in the continental United States. The city is rich in historic preservation and boasts more than 60 historic sites with many of them open to the public. St. Augustine is also home to many local attractions that offer education and entertainment to the entire family. There are always special events and activities being held. One of these events is our annual "Nights of Lights". Every year from early November until the end of January the downtown area is alive with millions of white Christmas lights. This is St. Augustine's version of a white Christmas. It is breathtaking and definitely worth a winter visit. Just a few miles from the historic downtown area are the St. Augustine beaches. The 24-mile stretch of beautiful beaches offers a wide array of activities. St. Augustine Beach is recognized as a destination for surfers and beach paddle tennis players as well as those who just like to swim or walk. The city and beach area are home to more than 150 restaurants boasting a diverse selection of food experiences ranging from our very fresh local seafood to traditional menus and of course, specialties from the Minorcan heritage that include the spicy and unique datil pepper seasoning.

Lighthouse Secrets is a compilation of recipes that reflect our casual lifestyle. The book contains recipes that incorporate the fresh seafood and vegetables that are St. Augustine. We have recipes that reflect the Minorcan heritage as well as some old family secrets and others that are simply our favorites. We have included a selection of recipes from some of our major fund-raising events. We hope you enjoy our special southern style, and we welcome you to St. Augustine and to our *Lighthouse Secrets*.

Lighthouse Secrets

Corporate Sponsors

The Junior Service League wishes to acknowledge and thank the following businesses and individuals whose generous support was instrumental in the creation of *Lighthouse Secrets*.

<u>Sponsors</u>
Prosperity Bank
Baker Pest Control

<u>Supporters</u>
Craig Funeral Home
Edmiston & Edmiston, PA
Elegant Events — Betty Crosby
Partel Consolidated Industries
Peggy Gachet — Watson Realty
William J. Oktavec, M.D. — San Agustin Eye Foundation

<u>Friends</u>
Adams Ink Invitations & Stationery

ATP Tour Charities

Dr. Jimmy Glenos, Specialist in Orthodontics

Neff Jewelers

New World Realty & Property Management, Inc.
Judi Schuyler & Irene Arriola

Mr. & Mrs. Kenneth Morse

Tara Regan Interiors

Karen M. Taylor, Land Planner

Standard Printing

Thomas H. Beach Farm, Inc.

Lighthouse Secrets

Acknowledgments

The Junior Service League of St. Augustine wishes to thank our members, families and friends whose contributions of recipes made this book possible.

Debbie Adams
Reinette Adams
Debbie Allred
Gail Andrews
Ann Aruanno
Vito Aruanno
Karen Atwell
Nancy Atwell
David Atwood
Jean A. Barns
M.L. Barrett
Marilyn Beach
Janet Berckmueller
Madeleine R. Bolz
Vivian Bosch
Barbara Bozard
Marianne Brinkhoff
Kate Brown
Ida Buckler
Nancy Burke
Cathy Burkhardt
Debbie Burkhardt
Jean Burmood
Agnes Butler
Kimberly A. Butner
Becca Cady
Bridget Carmichael

Imogene Carter
Edna Cartmel
Melinda Casado
Jean Chudoba
Kathy Chudoba
Mary M. Clukey
Sheri Cone
Betty Crosby
Anne Croxton
Eileen DeSotto
Deborah DeSotto
Mary Jane Dillon
Susan Dondero
Alex Farrimond
Anna Fisher
Andy Fleming
Beverly Fowdy
Carol Freudenberger
Peggy Gachet
Donnie Gader
Jane Garrett
Rita George
Susan Goedert
Jeanne Goedert
Ellie Goode
Priscilla Griggs
Tammy Grimes

Ingrid Guier
Sue Hale
Dianne Hale
Lynda Halstead
Sue Harroun
Malotte Hart
Jeanie Hartman
Kristen Hébert
Jackie Hird
Henry Hird
Lisa Hodgkins
Evelyn Hough
Sylvia Ingram
Kim Jeffs
Judy Johnson
Cheryl Johnson
Roberta Langley
  Johnson
Monica Jones
Donna Kehoe
Diane Key
Susie Keyser
Mona Langston
Mary Langworthy
Lorri Lassiter
Leslie LeBeau
Kim Lhota

Lighthouse Secrets

Karen Lichter
Esther Liming
Lee Livingston
Joan Maguire
Maureen Mann
Vee Markel
Scott Masson
Jane R. Masson
Lisa Masters
Donna Matthews
Jane Mathis
Malinda McCormick
Rachelle McCranie
Linda Meehan
Catherine Melton
Sara Mendenhall
Elsa Morales-Smith
Jayne Morgan
Dianne Morse
Kenneth Morse
Nancy Morse
Stephanie R. Nolt
Lynn O'Donnell-
   Stecker
Cheryl O'Steen
Kacki Oktavec
Colette Parker

Pat Parker
Louise B. Parker
Kevin Partel
Susan Partel
Mollie Pellicer
Michele R. Perry
Elaine Persons
Jeannie Pollard
Susan Ponder-Stansel
Lisa Priano
Joyce Rakers
Tara Regan
Kate Reynolds
W.V. Reynolds, M.D.
Kim Rockhill
Lois Rutherford
Elizabeth Schrum
Judi Schuyler
Becky Sejeck
Holly Sheppard
Nancy Sikes-Kline
Louise B. Smith
Kim Smith
Cindi Spalbi
Paula Steele
Holly Strickland
Jill Sulahain

Michelle Tasker
Diane Tausig
Judy Taylor
Karen Taylor
Jennifer Tesori
Brandy Thomas
Shelley Trela
Cathy Upchurch
Catalina Usina-Morse
Sarah R.
   VanOverwalle
Lisa Vassallo
Karen Volkman
Helen V. Wagner
Vicki Watkins
Chris Way
Donna Webb
Stevie Weimer
Virginia Whetstone
Shelly Whiteman
Denise Whitlock
Billie Williams
Anne Wolfe
Jane Wood
John Wood
Kathy Young

We sincerely hope that no one has been omitted. Please know that every-one who donated a recipe is deeply appreciated.

Lighthouse Secrets

Table of Contents

Appetizers

The City Gate

This is the only survivor of the gates that punctuated the Cubo and Rosario Lines that defended St. Augustine from invasion in colonial times.

The graceful coquina stone pillars, designed by royal engineer Manuel de Hita, have long survived the defense lines in which they were originally an opening.

In the early twentieth century, it was proposed to tear down the City Gate as an obstruction to traffic, prompting an early battle for historic preservation led by members of the Daughters of the American Revolution. That they were successful is evidenced by the fact that the pillars are still standing today.

They have been a proud symbol of St. Augustine and have often been copied elsewhere. In 1890 the famous architects McKim, Mead and White used them as a model for the Johnston Gate, the main entrance to Harvard Yard at the nation's oldest university in Cambridge, Massachusetts.

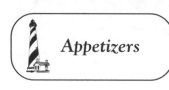

Appetizers

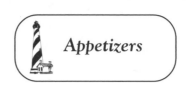
Tuna Mold

2 (6-ounce) cans solid white
    tuna in spring water, drained
    and flaked
1 (8-ounce) package cream
    cheese, softened
1 teaspoon lemon juice
2 teaspoons grated onion
1 teaspoon prepared horseradish
1 teaspoon Liquid Smoke
Dash of salt
Sliced almonds
Pimiento-stuffed olives

- Beat first 7 ingredients at medium speed with an electric mixer until creamy. Mold into a fish shape. Press almonds on sides to resemble scales; place olives as eyes. Chill. Serve with thin wheat crackers.

Yield: 20 servings

Crab-Stuffed Mushrooms

1 (7½-ounce) can lump
    crabmeat, drained
1½ tablespoons chopped fresh
    parsley
1 teaspoon chopped capers
¼ teaspoon dry mustard
½ cup mayonnaise
3 dozen large fresh mushrooms,
    stemmed

- Combine first 3 ingredients in a bowl. Combine mustard and mayonnaise, stirring well; add to crab mixture, tossing well. Fill each mushroom cap with 2 tablespoons crab mixture.
- Bake at 375° for 8 to 10 minutes or until thoroughly heated.

Yield: 3 dozen

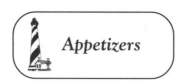

Cilantro-Lime Salsa

1 teaspoon salt
½ teaspoon ground red pepper
½ teaspoon ground white pepper
2 cups fresh corn kernels
1 red bell pepper, chopped
1 green bell pepper, chopped
2 tomatoes, diced
½ teaspoon minced garlic
½ bunch fresh parsley, chopped
1 bunch fresh cilantro, chopped
Juice of 6 limes
1 tablespoon olive oil
1 tablespoon balsamic vinegar

• Combine first 3 ingredients in a large bowl; add corn and next 9 ingredients, stirring well. Serve over fresh grilled seafood or in tortillas.

Yield: 20 to 40 servings (about 4 cups)

Crab Quesadillas

1 (10.5-ounce) package garlic and herb or other cheese spread
1 (8-ounce) package imitation crab chunks, chopped
1 (4.5-ounce) can chopped green chiles, drained
3 green onions, chopped
1 (4-ounce) can chopped pitted ripe olives
12 flour tortillas
2 tablespoons butter or margarine, melted

• Preheat oven to 375°.
• Combine first 5 ingredients, stirring well. Spread evenly on 6 tortillas to within ½ inch of edges. Top with remaining tortillas, and place in a single layer on 2 large cookie sheets. Brush tops with melted butter.
• Bake at 375° for 10 minutes or until edges are lightly browned and crisp. Let cool 1 minute. Cut into triangles, and serve warm with salsa and guacamole.

Yield: 24 servings

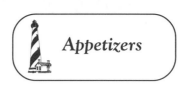

Caviar Pie

6 hard-cooked eggs, quartered

¼ cup butter or margarine, softened

1 teaspoon prepared mustard

¼ teaspoon salt

⅛ teaspoon pepper

1 teaspoon vinegar

½ cup chopped green onions

1 cup sour cream

1 (3-ounce) package cream cheese, softened

2 tablespoons chopped pimiento

1 (2-ounce) jar lumpfish caviar

Garnishes: lemon slices, pimiento strips

- Process first 6 ingredients in a food processor 15 to 30 seconds or until smooth, stopping to scrape down sides. Spread over the bottom of an 8-inch springform pan. Sprinkle evenly with green onions and chill at least 1 hour.
- Combine sour cream and cream cheese in a small bowl, stirring until smooth. Stir in chopped pimiento and spread over egg mixture. Chill 1 hour.
- Gently spoon caviar over cream cheese mixture. Garnish, if desired. Remove sides of pan and slice into 35 to 40 wedges. Spread on thinly sliced rye or pumpernickel bread.

Yield: 35 to 40 servings (1 [8-inch] pie)

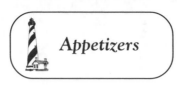
Pesto-Cheese Torte

3 cups fresh basil

6 garlic cloves, chopped

1 cup pine nuts or walnuts

1 cup extra-virgin olive oil

1½ cups freshly grated Parmesan cheese, divided

1 cup fresh breadcrumbs

½ cup butter or margarine, melted

4 (8-ounce) packages cream cheese, softened

4 large eggs

½ cup heavy cream

Garnish: sun-dried tomatoes packed in oil, drained and chopped

- Process first 3 ingredients in a food processor or blender until coarsely chopped (if using a blender process in 2 batches). With machine running, add oil in a slow, steady stream. Add 1 cup Parmesan cheese, and process until blended.
- Preheat oven to 325°.
- Combine remaining ½ cup Parmesan cheese, breadcrumbs, and butter, tossing to blend. Press into the bottom of an 8-inch springform pan.
- Bake at 325° for 5 to 10 minutes.
- Beat cream cheese at medium speed with an electric mixer until smooth; add 2 cups pesto, eggs, and cream, beating well. Pour into prepared pan.
- Bake at 325° for 1 hour or until set. Chill.
- Run a knife around edges of pan; remove sides. Garnish, if desired, and serve with bagel chips.

Yield: about 30 servings

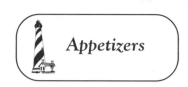
Pork Slices and Sesame Seeds

1 to 1½ pounds pork tenderloin
Salt and pepper to taste
Hot Dijon or hot Chinese
  mustard
3 tablespoons sesame seeds

- Season tenderloin with salt and pepper to taste, and place in a roasting pan.
- Bake at 350° for 40 minutes or until done. Let cool. Slice thinly, and arrange on a serving platter.
- Bake sesame seeds on a baking sheet at 350° for 2 to 3 minutes or until toasted, watching closely so as not to burn. Place sesame seeds and mustard in separate small serving bowls. Place bowls on serving tray with tenderloin slices.

Yield: 12 servings

Guests should dip the tenderloin slices in mustard first and then in sesame seeds.

Roasted Sweet Red Pepper in Balsamic Vinegar

1 large block Monterey Jack
  cheese, sliced the size of the
  crackers
1 (12-ounce) jar roasted sweet
  red peppers, drained and thinly
  sliced
1 bottle balsamic vinegar

- Place cheese slices on a large serving platter with an edge; place a piece of red pepper on each cheese slice. Sprinkle with balsamic vinegar. Serve with whole wheat crackers.

Yield: about 30 servings

The balsamic vinegar makes this dish!

Artichoke Squares

2 (6-ounce) jars marinated
  artichoke hearts
1 onion, chopped
1 garlic clove, minced
4 large eggs
¼ cup Italian-seasoned
  breadcrumbs
Dash of hot sauce
½ teaspoon dried oregano
Salt and pepper to taste
2 cups (8 ounces) shredded
  Cheddar cheese

- Drain the liquid from 1 jar artichoke hearts into a skillet; add onion and garlic, and sauté in hot liquid until tender.
- Drain remaining artichoke hearts, discarding liquid; chop all artichoke hearts.
- Whisk eggs in a large bowl; add breadcrumbs and next 3 ingredients, stirring well. Stir in onion, garlic, artichoke, and cheese, mixing well. Spoon into a 7 x 11 x 2-inch pan.
- Bake at 325° for 30 minutes. Cut into squares, and serve hot.

Yield: about 30 squares

Marinated Havarti

8 ounces Havarti cheese, cut into
  ½-inch cubes
½ medium-size red bell pepper,
  cut into strips
½ cup pimiento-stuffed olives
⅔ cup olive oil
⅓ cup white wine vinegar
1 teaspoon dried oregano
1 teaspoon dried crushed red
  pepper
½ teaspoon dried thyme
1 garlic clove, quartered

- Place first 3 ingredients in a 1-quart airtight container.
- Cook oil and next 5 ingredients in a saucepan over medium heat, stirring often, until thoroughly heated. Let cool. Pour over cheese mixture, and seal. Toss to coat. Chill up to 5 days.

Yield: 8 servings

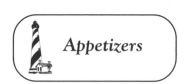
Spinach Squares

1½ (10-ounce) packages frozen
   chopped spinach, cooked and
   well drained
4 cups (16 ounces) shredded
   Cheddar cheese
¾ cup chopped onion
2 garlic cloves, minced
1 cup all-purpose flour
1 teaspoon baking powder
1 teaspoon salt
2 large eggs, lightly beaten
1 cup milk
¼ cup butter or margarine,
   melted
Dash of Worcestershire sauce

- Preheat oven to 350°.
- Combine spinach, cheese,
  onion, and garlic in a bowl.
- Combine flour, baking powder,
  and salt in a large bowl. Add
  eggs and next 3 ingredients,
  stirring well. Add spinach
  mixture, stirring well. Spoon
  into a greased 9 x 13 x 2-inch
  pan.
- Bake at 350° for 35 minutes. Let
  cool slightly, and cut into 1-inch
  squares.

Yield: 12 servings

*This appetizer can be frozen and reheated without thawing. Bake at
300° for 15 minutes.*

Festive Cheese Appetizer

4 cups (16 ounces) shredded
   Cheddar cheese
1 cup chopped pecans
1 cup mayonnaise
1 small onion, chopped
Dash of pepper
Strawberry preserves

- Combine first 5 ingredients,
  stirring well; shape into a ring.
  Chill.
- Fill center of cheese ring with
  preserves, and serve with
  gourmet crackers.

Pizza Primavera

2 packages refrigerated crescent
    rolls

2 (8-ounce) packages cream
    cheese, softened

¾ cup mayonnaise

½ teaspoon garlic powder or
    garlic salt

1 onion, finely chopped

3 large tomatoes, thinly sliced
    and drained on paper towels

3 carrots, finely chopped or
    shredded

1 green, red, or yellow bell
    pepper, finely chopped

½ cup grated Parmesan cheese

- Unroll crescent roll dough, and fit into a 10 x 15-inch jelly-roll pan, pressing seams to seal and covering entire pan.
- Bake at 375° for 10 to 12 minutes or until golden brown. Let cool.
- Combine cream cheese and next 3 ingredients, stirring well; spread over cooled pastry, leaving a narrow border on all sides. Sprinkle with tomato, carrot, and bell pepper. Sprinkle with Parmesan cheese. Cover with plastic wrap, and chill at least overnight.
- Cut pizza into 1-inch squares, and cover with plastic wrap until ready to serve.

Yield: 12 servings

Crabmeat Points

½ cup butter or margarine

1 jar Cheddar cheese spread

3 dashes of Worcestershire sauce

1 (6½-ounce) can king crabmeat,
    drained and flaked

6 English muffins, halved

- Melt butter in a saucepan over medium heat; add cheese spread, and cook until melted. Stir in Worcestershire sauce and crabmeat. Remove from heat, and let stand 10 minutes.
- Spread crab mixture evenly on muffin halves. Freeze. Cut each frozen muffin half into eighths. Broil on a baking sheet until cheese is browned.

Yield: 8 dozen

Caponata

2 large eggplants, peeled and cut into 1-inch cubes

3 cups onion, coarsely chopped

1½ cups coarsely chopped bell pepper

1½ cups coarsely chopped celery

½ cup olive oil

1 (8-ounce) can tomato sauce

1 (6-ounce) can tomato paste

5 garlic cloves, minced

6 ounces pitted ripe olives

½ cup pitted green olives

3 tablespoons sugar

¼ cup capers

1½ teaspoons dried oregano

1 tablespoon salt

• Cover eggplant with salt water, and let stand 20 minutes; drain and rinse.

• Combine onion and next 3 ingredients in a microwave-safe 4-quart baking dish. Cover with wax paper, and microwave at HIGH for 30 minutes, stirring twice. Stir in eggplant and cook, covered, at HIGH 30 minutes, stirring once. Stir in tomato sauce and tomato paste and cook, covered, at HIGH 10 minutes. Stir in garlic and next 6 ingredients and cook, covered, at HIGH 5 minutes. Chill. Serve with crackers or French bread slices.

Yield: 2 quarts

Aunt Franki's Vegetable Dip

1 cup mayonnaise

1 cup sour cream

1 (3-ounce) package cream cheese, softened

2 tablespoons minced green onions

2 tablespoons Beau Monde seasoning or celery salt

1 (10-ounce) package frozen chopped spinach, thawed and well drained

• Combine all ingredients, stirring well. Chill.

Yield: 8 to 12 servings

Tortilla Ham Rolls

1 package 10-inch flour tortillas

2 (8-ounce) packages cream cheese, softened

Dijon mustard

12 to 16 ounces thinly sliced deli ham

1 (12-ounce) package finely shredded Monterey Jack or mild Cheddar cheese

Chopped fresh chives (optional)

1 jar sweet pepper relish, well drained

- Spread 1 tortilla with a thin layer of cream cheese; top with a thin layer of mustard. Top with 2 thin layers of ham; sprinkle with cheese and, if desired, chives. Sprinkle evenly with relish. Roll up tightly, and secure with wooden picks while you wrap tightly with plastic wrap.
- Repeat procedure with each remaining tortilla and remaining ingredients. Chill 8 to 24 hours. Slice and serve.

Yield: 12 servings

Be sure to use sweet pepper relish not sweet pickle relish.

Crab Dip

1 (8-ounce) package cream cheese, softened

¼ cup sour cream

1 tablespoon finely chopped onion

¼ teaspoon pepper

1¼ teaspoons hot sauce (or to taste)

1 small can lump crabmeat, drained

Garnish: chopped fresh chives

- Beat cream cheese and sour cream at medium speed with a hand held mixer until creamy; add onion, pepper, and hot sauce, beating well. Fold in crabmeat. Serve chilled or bake in a baking dish at 350° until bubbly; garnish, if desired. Serve with crackers, bread, or toast.

Yield: 8 to 12 servings

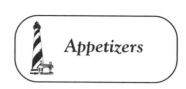

Pixie Kitchen Clam Dip

1 (8-ounce) package cream
    cheese, softened
8 ounces minced clams
1 tablespoon mayonnaise
½ teaspoon garlic salt
1 tablespoon Worcestershire
    sauce

- Combine all ingredients in a
  bowl, stirring well. Chill several
  days.

Yield: 8 to 12 servings

Chilling the dip several days allows the flavors to blend.

Bacon Rolls

White bread slices
1 (10¾-ounce) can cream of
    mushroom soup, undiluted
Bacon slices

- Spread bread slices with soup;
  remove crusts, and cut each slice
  into 3 strips. Wrap each strip
  with a bacon slice, and secure
  with wooden picks.
- Bake at 325° for 25 minutes.

Yield: 10 to 12 servings

Quick Hummus

1 or 2 garlic cloves
1 (15-ounce) can garbanzo
    beans, drained
¼ cup tahini
2 tablespoons lemon juice
2 tablespoons water
Salt and pepper to taste

- Pulse garlic in a food processor
  1 or 2 times or until chopped.
  Add garbanzo beans and next
  4 ingredients, and process until
  smooth. Serve with assorted raw
  vegetables.

Yield: 1⅓ cups

Guacamole

1 large or 2 small ripe avocados

2 to 3 tablespoons whipped
   cream cheese

½ teaspoon lemon juice

1 teaspoon garlic salt or garlic
   powder

1 (4-ounce) can chopped green
   chiles, drained

2 to 3 tablespoons medium or
   mild green taco sauce

4 to 6 drops hot sauce

1 small tomato, chopped

• Peel avocados, and mash in a
bowl with a fork until smooth.
Add cream cheese, lemon juice,
and garlic salt, stirring well. Add
chiles, taco sauce, and hot sauce,
stirring well. Gently fold in
tomato. Refrigerate just until
chilled; serve immediately.

Yield: 8 to 12 servings

Smoked Salmon Spread

1 (15½-ounce) can red salmon,
   drained and boned

1 (8-ounce) package fat-free
   cream cheese

1 tablespoon prepared
   horseradish

1 tablespoon grated onion

1 tablespoon lemon juice

⅛ teaspoon Liquid Smoke

1 tablespoon chopped fresh
   parsley

• Stir together first 6 ingredients
in a medium bowl. Transfer to a
serving bowl; cover and chill.
Sprinkle with chopped parsley,
and serve with low-fat whole
wheat crackers.

Yield: 16 servings

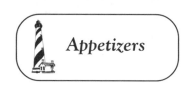
St. Augustine Sweet Onion Sandwiches

2 loaves Pepperidge Farm Thin Sliced sandwich bread or Arnold's Thin Sliced sandwich bread

Mayonnaise

3 (4-ounce) containers garlic and herb cheese spread or equal amount of softened cream cheese with chives

Several pounds St. Augustine or Vidalia Sweet Onions, very thinly sliced

Salt and pepper to taste

2 packages fresh parsley, minced

- Cut bread slices into rounds using a cookie cutter; cover slices with damp paper towels to keep moist.
- Spread 1 side of half of bread slices with a thin layer of mayonnaise; spread 1 side of remaining bread slices with a thin layer of cheese spread. Place 1 onion slice on each mayonnaise-coated bread slice; sprinkle with salt and pepper; top each with a cheese spread-coated slice, cheese side down. Lightly spread sides of sandwiches with mayonnaise, and roll in parsley.
- Stack sandwiches in layers in a deep pan, covering each layer with damp paper towels and separating layers with wax paper or plastic wrap. Cover tightly, and chill overnight.

Yield: 20 servings

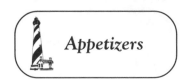

Skewered Chicken

1½ pounds chicken breasts,
   skinned and boned
1 tablespoon balsamic or red
   wine vinegar
⅓ cup white or red wine
½ cup chopped chutney
¼ cup olive oil
3 green and yellow bell peppers,
   cut into ½-inch squares

• Cut chicken into ¾-inch cubes.
Combine vinegar and next 3
ingredients in a shallow dish,
stirring well; add chicken and
bell pepper, tossing to coat.
Chill overnight. Drain chicken
and bell pepper, discarding
marinade. Thread chicken and
bell pepper alternately on metal
skewers.
• Grill skewers over medium heat
(300° to 350°), turning
occasionally, 10 minutes.

Yield: 6 to 8 servings

Chicken Curry Balls

4 ounces cream cheese, softened
2 tablespoons mayonnaise
1 cup chopped cooked chicken
1 cup blanched sliced almonds
1 tablespoon curry powder
1 tablespoon finely chopped
   chutney
½ teaspoon salt
½ cup chopped green onions
½ cup flaked coconut, toasted

• Combine cream cheese and
mayonnaise in a bowl, stirring
until blended. Add chicken and
next 5 ingredients, stirring well.
Chill 4 hours. Shape into 1-inch
balls, and roll in coconut. Serve
chilled.

Yield: 8 to 10 servings

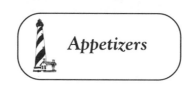

Dill-Sour Cream Dip

1 cup sour cream
½ cup mayonnaise
1½ tablespoons finely chopped
  green onions
2 teaspoons dried parsley flakes,
  crushed
1 teaspoon dried dill weed
1 teaspoon seasoned salt

• Combine first 6 ingredients,
stirring well. Cover and chill
several hours. Serve with
crackers or assorted raw
vegetables.

Yield: about 1½ cups

Cold Black-Eyed Pea Dip

2 (15-ounce) cans black-eyed
  peas, drained
1 red bell pepper, chopped
1 can yellow corn kernels,
  drained
3 celery ribs, chopped
1 purple onion, chopped
½ cup olive oil
¼ cup red wine
2 bacon slices, cooked and
  crumbled
Dash of dried parsley flakes
Dash of dried oregano
1 teaspoon Dijon mustard

• Combine first 11 ingredients in a
bowl, stirring well. Chill 3 days.
Serve with tortilla chips.

Yield: 12 to 14 servings

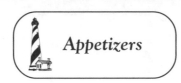

Crabmeat Spread

1 (6½-ounce) can king crabmeat,
   drained and flaked
½ cup butter or margarine
3 hard-cooked eggs, chopped
¼ cup mayonnaise
2 to 4 tablespoons chopped onion

• Combine first 5 ingredients,
stirring well; spoon into a
serving bowl. Chill several
hours. Let stand at room
temperature 30 to 60 minutes
before serving. Serve with
crackers.

Yield: 8 servings

Spirited Apricot Brie

½ cup apricot jam
1 tablespoon grated orange rind
1 tablespoon brandy or fresh
   orange juice
1 tablespoon lemon juice
⅛ teaspoon ground cinnamon
1 (8-ounce) Brie cheese slice or
   wheel

• Combine first 5 ingredients in a
small microwave-safe serving
dish. Microwave, covered, at
HIGH 1 to 1½ minutes or until
bubbly. Place Brie on sauce.
Cook, uncovered, at HIGH
1 minute, checking after
30 seconds.

Yield: 8 servings

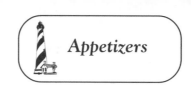
Marinated Spiced Shrimp with Herbs

3½ to 4 pounds unpeeled, large fresh shrimp

3 or 4 garlic cloves

2½ cups red or white wine vinegar

1 cup water

1 cup vegetable oil

¾ cup olive oil

½ cup chopped fresh or ¼ cup dried parsley

3 tablespoons salt

2 teaspoons black pepper

3 tablespoons dry mustard

2 teaspoons dried oregano

2 teaspoons dried thyme

2 teaspoons dried rosemary

2 teaspoons dried basil

¼ cup sugar

1 purple onion, halved and very thinly sliced

1 red bell pepper, very thinly sliced

1 yellow bell pepper, very thinly sliced

- Bring a large pot of water to a boil; add shrimp, and return to a boil. Turn off heat. Let stand 1 minute or until shrimp turn pink; drain. Rinse with cold water to stop the cooking process. Peel shrimp and devein (see note).
- Process garlic in a food processor until finely chopped; add vinegar to wash down sides. Pour garlic and vinegar into a large bowl; add 1 cup water and next 11 ingredients, whisking well.
- Combine shrimp, onion, and bell peppers; place evenly in heavy-duty zip-top plastic bags. Pour marinade evenly into bags; seal and turn to coat. Chill 36 to 48 hours, turning occasionally.

Yield: 20 to 30 servings

Three bottles Paul Newman's olive oil and wine vinegar dressing may be substituted for wine vinegar, 1 cup water, and oils; add a small amount to wash down food processor bowl sides, and combine with remaining dressing, parsley, and next 8 ingredients in large bowl. Proceed as directed.
To peel and devein shrimp, carefully pull away shell so as not to tear flesh. With a sharp knife, score the center of the outer curve making a ¹⁄₁₆-inch incision the length of the shrimp. Carefully remove the vein with the tip of the knife or your fingertips. Some shrimp will have a vein on the underside as well. Rinse under running water to remove sand.

Salmon Ball

1 (16-ounce) can salmon,
  drained and boned

¼ teaspoon Liquid Smoke

1 (8-ounce) package cream
  cheese, softened

2 tablespoons finely chopped
  onion

1 tablespoon lemon juice

2 teaspoons prepared horseradish

¼ teaspoon salt

1 cup pecans, chopped

½ cup fresh parsley, finely
  chopped

• Combine first 7 ingredients,
  stirring well. Chill at least 1
  hour. Shape into a ball, and roll
  in nuts and parsley. Serve with
  crackers or toasted pita triangles.

Yield: 8 servings

Shrimp Dip

1 can tomato soup, undiluted

1 envelope unflavored gelatin

¼ cup cold water

1 (8-ounce) package cream
  cheese, softened

1 cup mayonnaise

Dash of salt

¾ cup finely chopped celery

½ cup finely chopped green bell
  pepper

½ cup finely chopped onion

2 cans shrimp or 1 pound fresh
  shrimp, cooked and chopped

• Bring soup to a boil in a
  saucepan. Combine gelatin and
  ¼ cup cold water. Let stand
  5 minutes.

• Combine soup, gelatin, cream
  cheese, and next 6 ingredients,
  stirring well. Spoon mixture into
  an greased mold. Chill until set.
  Invert onto a serving plate.

Yield: 12 servings

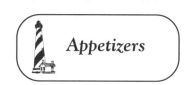

Black-Eyed Pea and Bell Pepper Caviar

2 (15-ounce) cans black-eyed peas, rinsed and drained

1 (15-ounce) can black-eyed peas with jalapeños, rinsed and drained

2 medium tomatoes, seeded and chopped

¾ cup chopped onion

½ cup chopped yellow bell pepper

½ cup chopped green bell pepper

¼ cup chopped seeded jalapeño pepper

½ teaspoon minced garlic

½ teaspoon ground cumin

¼ teaspoon pepper

This recipe can be prepared ahead.

• Combine first 10 ingredients in a large bowl, stirring well. Cover and chill at least 2 hours. Serve with large corn or tortilla chips.

Yield: 8 cups

Beau Catcher

1 (8-ounce) package cream cheese, softened

1 tablespoon mayonnaise

¼ teaspoon garlic powder

¼ teaspoon onion powder

½ teaspoon prepared horseradish

1 to 2 tablespoons milk

• Combine first 5 ingredients in a bowl, stirring with a fork until smooth. Stir in milk, thinning to desired consistency. Serve with potato chips or crackers.

Yield: 8 servings

Sun-Dried Tomato Dip

2 garlic bulbs
Olive oil
1 (8-ounce) package cream
   cheese, softened
4 ounces feta cheese
Chopped fresh basil to taste
½ cup sun-dried tomatoes packed
   in oil, chopped

- Slice the bottom off of the garlic bulbs, and place bulbs on aluminum foil; drizzle with a small amount of olive oil, and seal.
- Bake at 425° for 45 minutes.
- Remove garlic from oven, and squeeze pulp into a bowl. Add cream cheese and feta to garlic pulp, and beat with a hand held mixer until smooth. Add basil and dried tomatoes, beating well. Mold into desired shape, and chill. Serve with Melba toast or crackers.

Yield: 8 to 12 servings

Dill-Artichoke Dip

½ cup grated Parmesan cheese,
   divided
11 ounces Neufchâtel cheese
½ cup fat-free cream cheese
½ cup mayonnaise
2 (6-ounce) jars marinated
   artichoke hearts, well drained
   and chopped
½ cup toasted nuts
2 green onions, chopped
1½ tablespoons all-purpose flour
2 teaspoons chopped fresh dill
¾ cup soft whole wheat
   breadcrumbs
1 tablespoon butter or margarine,
   melted

- Beat ¼ cup Parmesan cheese and next 3 ingredients at low speed with an electric mixer until smooth; stir in artichoke and next 4 ingredients. Spoon into an ungreased shallow 1½-quart baking dish. Combine remaining ¼ cup Parmesan cheese, breadcrumbs, and melted butter, stirring well; sprinkle over dip.
- Bake at 350° for 20 minutes. Serve hot with crackers.

Yield: 12 servings

Breads, Beverages & Brunch

The Oldest Wooden Schoolhouse

There were many wooden buildings in colonial St. Augustine, but this is the only one we know of that has survived.

Originally built as a private residence in the early 1800s, 14 St. George Street has spent the past century in commercial use as a photography studio, art gallery, tea shoppe, and—for many decades—a tourist attraction called "The Oldest Wooden Schoolhouse."

It escaped a proposal to tear it down in 1942, and survived to serve as the backdrop in 1998 to a rally for Jeb Bush as he campaigned for governor of Florida.

Breads, Brunch & Beverages

Scones

2 cups all-purpose flour
3 tablespoons baking powder
½ teaspoon salt
2 tablespoons sugar
⅓ cup butter or margarine, cut up
¾ cup milk

- Preheat oven to 425°.
- Sift together first 4 ingredients; cut in butter with a pastry blender until crumbly; stir in milk. Knead dough 15 times. Roll to 1-inch thickness on a lightly floured surface. Cut with a round cookie cutter and place scones on a baking sheet.
- Bake at 425° for 10 to 15 minutes.

Yield: 1 dozen

Yorkshire Pudding

1 teaspoon salt
1¾ cups milk
¼ cup water
3 large eggs
1 cup all-purpose flour
Shortening

- Beat first 4 ingredients with a wooden spoon until smooth. Combine flour and a small amount of liquid in a bowl, stirring well; gradually work in remaining liquid.
- Place a small amount of shortening in each muffin pan cup. Place in a cold oven; preheat oven to 425°. Ladle pudding into muffin cups, filling half full.
- Bake at 425° for 5 minutes. Reduce oven temperature to 375° (do not open oven door), and bake 30 minutes.

Yield: 10 to 12 servings

Sunshine Yeast Bread

1 (¼-ounce) envelope active dry yeast or 1 cake compressed yeast

¼ cup warm water (use lukewarm water for yeast cake)

1 cup milk, scalded

⅓ cup sugar

½ cup shortening

1 teaspoon salt

5 to 5½ cups sifted enriched flour

2 large eggs, lightly beaten

2 tablespoons grated orange rind

¼ cup fresh orange juice

Powdered sugar

Fresh orange juice

Dough may also be formed into loaves and baked in 2 (5 x 9-inch) loaf pans.

- Combine yeast and ¼ cup warm water; let stand 5 minutes.
- Beat milk and next 3 ingredients at medium speed with an electric mixer until blended; let cool until lukewarm. Stir in 2 cups flour beating well. Add eggs beating well. Stir in yeast mixture. Stir in remaining flour, orange rind, and ¼ cup juice to make a soft dough. Let rise in a warm place (85°), free from drafts, 10 minutes.
- Knead dough 5 to 10 minutes on a lightly floured surface until smooth and elastic. Place in a lightly greased bowl, turning to grease top. Cover and let rise in a warm place, free from drafts, 2 hours or until doubled in bulk. Punch dough down; cover and let rest 10 minutes.
- Roll dough into a ½-inch-thick rectangle on a lightly floured surface. Cut into ½-inch-wide strips, and roll strips between your hands to smooth. Twist each strip and place on cookie sheet. If preferred, roll into a ball for a more traditional roll.
- Bake at 375° for 15 minutes.
- Combine powdered sugar and orange juice to make a glaze. Remove rolls from oven, and brush generously with glaze, if desired.

Yield: 12 rolls

Breads

Doughnuts

2 cups lukewarm water
2 (¼-ounce) envelopes active dry
   yeast
1 cup sugar
1½ teaspoons salt
1 large egg
¼ cup shortening
6½ to 7 cups all-purpose flour,
   sifted
Powdered sugar (optional)

- Combine 2 cups lukewarm water and yeast in a large bowl; add sugar, beating at medium speed with an electric mixer. Add salt, egg, and shortening, beating well. Gradually stir in flour to form a dough. Knead dough well. Place in a lightly greased bowl, turning to grease top. Cover and let rise in a warm place (85°), free from drafts, 1½ to 2 hours.
- Punch dough down. Roll to ¼-inch thickness on a lightly floured surface. Cut out with a doughnut cutter. Place doughnuts and "holes" on a cloth in a warm place. Cover and let rise 1 hour.
- Heat oil in a large deep-fryer to 370°. Cook doughnuts, 4 or 5 at a time (do not let overlap), 1 to 1½ minutes on each side or until golden brown. (Doughnut "holes" brown faster.) Let drain and cool on paper towels. Sprinkle with powdered sugar, if desired.

Yield: 3 dozen

Cream Cheese and Chocolate Danish

4 to 5 cups all-purpose flour,
   divided

¾ cup sugar, divided

1 teaspoon salt

2 (¼-ounce) envelopes active dry
   yeast

½ cup milk

½ cup water

¼ cup butter or margarine

2 large eggs, at room temperature

1 (8-ounce) package cream
   cheese, softened

1 egg yolk

Favorite chocolate frosting

• Combine ¼ cup flour, ½ cup
  sugar, salt, and yeast in a large
  bowl.
• Heat milk, ½ cup water, and
  butter in a small saucepan over
  low heat until warm (butter
  needn't melt). Gradually add to
  dry ingredients, beating at
  medium speed with an electric
  mixer 2 minutes. Add 2 eggs and
  ½ cup flour, beating until batter
  is thick. Beat at high speed
  2 minutes. Stir in enough
  remaining flour to make a soft
  dough.
• Knead dough 8 minutes or until
  smooth and elastic. Place in a
  greased bowl, turning to grease
  top. Cover and let rise in a warm
  place (85°), free from drafts,
  1 hour or until doubled in bulk.
• Beat cream cheese and
  remaining ¼ cup sugar at
  medium speed with an electric
  mixer until light and fluffy. Add
  egg yolk, beating well.
• Punch dough down. Roll one-
  fourth of dough into a rectangle
  on a lightly floured surface.
  Spread with one-fourth of cream
  cheese mixture. Roll up, jelly
  roll fashion, pressing edges to
  seal. Repeat process three times
  with remaining dough and
  cream cheese. Cut slits in each

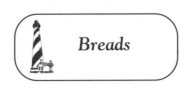
(Cream Cheese and Chocolate Danish continued)

loaf at 1-inch intervals. Cover and let rise in a warm place, free from drafts, 1 hour.
- Bake at 350° for 20 to 25 minutes. Let cool. Spread evenly with chocolate frosting.

Yield: 4 loaves

Apple-Nut Coffee Cake

½ cup shortening
1 cup granulated sugar
2 large eggs
1 teaspoon vanilla extract
2 cups all-purpose flour
1 teaspoon baking soda
1 teaspoon baking powder
¼ teaspoon salt
1 cup sour cream
2 cups chopped apple
½ cup chopped nuts
½ cup firmly packed brown sugar
1 teaspoon ground cinnamon
2 tablespoons butter or margarine, melted

- Beat shortening and granulated sugar at medium speed with an electric mixer until creamy; add eggs and vanilla, beating well.
- Sift together flour and next 3 ingredients; add to creamed mixture alternately with sour cream, beating well after each addition. Fold in apples. Spread batter in a greased 9 x 13 x 2-inch pan.
- Combine nuts and next 3 ingredients; sprinkle over batter.
- Bake at 350° for 35 to 40 minutes.

Yield: 12 servings

Breads

Delicious Mini Biscuits

½ cup butter
½ cup margarine
1 cup sour cream
2½ cups self-rising flour

- Combine all ingredients, stirring well. Spoon batter into miniature muffin pan cups (do not smooth tops).
- Bake at 350° for 20 minutes. Serve warm.

Yield: 2 dozen

Pineapple-Zucchini Bread

3 large eggs
2 cups sugar
1 cup vegetable oil
1 teaspoon vanilla
2 cups shredded unpeeled zucchini
1 (8¼-ounce) can crushed pineapple, drained
3 cups all-purpose flour
2 teaspoons baking soda
½ teaspoon baking powder
1 teaspoon salt
1½ teaspoons ground cinnamon
¾ teaspoon ground nutmeg
1 cup chopped walnuts

- Beat first 4 ingredients at medium speed with an electric mixer until thick and foamy. Stir in zucchini and pineapple.
- Combine flour and next 6 ingredients; add to zucchini mixture, stirring just until moistened. Pour batter into 2 lightly greased 5 x 9-inch loaf pans or 4 small loaf pans.
- Bake at 350° for 60 minutes (bake small loaves 40 minutes).

Yield: 2 to 4 loaves

Poppy Seed Bread

1½ cups vegetable oil
2½ cups sugar
3 large eggs
1½ cups milk
3 cups all-purpose flour
1½ teaspoons baking powder
1 teaspoon salt
3 tablespoons poppy seeds
1 teaspoon butter extract
1 teaspoon vanilla extract
1½ teaspoons almond extract

- Beat oil and sugar at medium speed with an electric mixer until blended; add eggs, beating well. Add milk and next 7 ingredients, beating well. Pour batter into a lightly greased 5 x 9-inch loaf pan or 2 small loaf pans.
- Bake at 350° for 1 hour.

Yield: 1 or 2 loaves

Lemon Bread

1 (18.25-ounce) package lemon cake mix
1 (3⅜-ounce) package vanilla or lemon instant pudding mix
1 cup water
½ cup vegetable oil
4 large eggs
½ cup powdered sugar
3 tablespoons lemon juice

- Beat first 5 ingredients at medium speed with an electric mixer 5 minutes. Pour batter into 2 greased 5 x 9-inch loaf pans.
- Bake at 350° for 40 to 50 minutes.
- Combine sugar and lemon juice, stirring until smooth. Remove bread from oven and pour glaze over hot bread.

Yield: 2 loaves

This is a good substitute for pound cake. It is best if frozen before served. It can be served as a dessert or as a breakfast coffee cake.

For a low-fat version, substitute ½ cup applesauce for oil and 1 cup egg substitute for eggs.

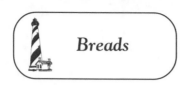

Banana Nut Bread

½ cup shortening

1 cup sugar

3 ripe bananas, mashed

2 large eggs

2 cups all-purpose flour

1 teaspoon baking soda

¼ teaspoon salt

Dash of ground nutmeg

Dash of ground cinnamon

Dash of ground cloves

1 cup chopped walnuts or pecans

- Preheat oven to 325°.
- Beat shortening and sugar at medium speed with an electric mixer until creamy; add eggs, 1 at a time, beating well after each addition. Stir in bananas.
- Combine flour and next 5 ingredients; add to creamed mixture, beating just until moistened. Stir in nuts. Pour batter into a lightly greased wax paper-lined 5 x 9-inch loaf pan or 2 small loaf pans.
- Bake at 325° for 1 hour.

Yield: 1 or 2 loaves

Cranberry Bread

2 cups all-purpose flour

1½ teaspoons baking powder

½ teaspoon baking soda

1 teaspoon salt

¾ cup sugar

½ cup chopped pecans

1 cup fresh or frozen cranberries, chopped

1 large egg, lightly beaten

¾ cup orange juice

2 tablespoons vegetable oil

- Preheat oven to 350°.
- Sift together first 5 ingredients; stir in nuts and cranberries. Combine cranberry mixture, egg, juice, and oil; beat at medium speed with an electric mixer until blended. Pour batter into a greased and floured 5 x 9-inch loaf pan.
- Bake at 350° for 50 minutes or until golden brown.

Yield: 1 loaf

Breads

Honey Wheat Rolls

2 (¼-ounce) envelopes active dry
   yeast
1 tablespoon salt
4 cups all-purpose flour
⅓ cup honey
3 tablespoons butter
2½ cups hot water
3 cups whole wheat flour
Vegetable oil

- Combine yeast, salt, and 2 cups all-purpose flour in a large bowl; add honey, butter, and 2½ cups hot water, and beat at medium speed with an electric mixer 2 minutes. Add 1 cup all-purpose flour and ½ cup whole wheat flour, and beat 1 minute. Add remaining flour, stirring until dough is soft and sticky.
- Turn dough out onto a lightly floured surface, and knead 5 to 10 minutes, adding flour as needed until dough is smooth and elastic. Cover with plastic wrap and a towel. Let stand at room temperature 20 minutes.
- Punch dough down, and divide into 24 equal portions. Divide each portions into thirds, and roll into balls. Place 3 small balls into each greased muffin pan cup. Brush tops lightly with oil. Cover with plastic wrap and chill 2 to 24 hours.
- Preheat oven to 400°.
- Let stand at room temperature 10 minutes before baking. Remove plastic wrap and bake at 400° for 15 minutes.

Yield: 2 dozen

This is a great make-ahead recipe.

Italian Herb Bread

1 (¼-ounce) envelope active dry
  yeast
1 cup lukewarm water
1 cup scalded milk
3 tablespoons granulated sugar
2½ teaspoons salt
2½ teaspoons shortening
6 cups sifted all-purpose flour
½ teaspoon dried thyme
½ teaspoon dried oregano
½ teaspoon dried basil

- Sprinkle yeast over 1 cup lukewarm water in a large bowl, stirring to dissolve.
- Combine milk and next 3 ingredients. Add milk mixture, 3 cups flour, and next 3 ingredients to yeast mixture, beating at medium speed with an electric mixer until smooth. Stir in enough remaining flour to make a dough. Turn out onto a lightly floured surface and knead until smooth. Place in a lightly greased bowl, turning to grease top. Let rise in a warm place (85°), free from drafts, until doubled in bulk.
- Divide dough in half, and shape into loaves. Place in 2 (5 x 9-inch) loaf pans.
- Bake at 400° for 50 minutes.

Yield: 2 loaves

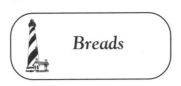
Garlic Bubble Bread

½ to ¾ cup butter or margarine, melted

2 or 3 garlic cloves, minced

1 teaspoon salt-free garlic and herb seasoning

1 recipe Refrigerator Bread Dough

¾ cup grated Parmesan cheese

- Combine first 3 ingredients in a shallow bowl.
- Form dough into a roll 18 inches long; cut into 30 equal pieces, and form into balls. Dip each ball in butter mixture, and roll in cheese, reserving remaining butter mixture and cheese.
- Place balls ½ inch apart in a 5 x 9-inch loaf pan or a 9-inch tube pan. Arrange a second layer of balls on top of first layer. Cover and let rise in a warm place (85°), free from drafts, until top of loaf is slightly higher than pan. Brush lightly with remaining melted butter and sprinkle with remaining cheese.
- Bake at 375° for 30 minutes. Serve uncut; break off pieces individually at the table.

Yield: 1 loaf

For a variation, substitute cinnamon and sugar for garlic, herb seasoning, and cheese; serve as a breakfast coffee cake.

Refrigerator Bread Dough

¾ cup scalded milk
6 tablespoons sugar
1 tablespoon salt
5 tablespoons shortening
½ cup warm water
2 (¼-ounce) envelopes active dry
  yeast
1 large egg, lightly beaten
4½ cups all-purpose flour

- Combine first 4 ingredients; let cool to lukewarm.
- Combine ½ cup warm water and yeast in a large bowl, stirring to dissolve. Stir in milk mixture. Add egg and 2 cups flour, beating with an electric mixer until smooth. Stir in remaining 2½ cups flour to form a dough. Place in a lightly greased bowl, turning to grease top. Cover tightly with plastic wrap and chill 2 hours or up to 2 to 3 days.
- Use dough as needed. Punch dough down, and cut off as needed.

Bloody Mary Mix

1 (46-ounce) can clamato juice
1 (46-ounce) can vegetable juice
2 teaspoons salt
2 teaspoons pepper
2 teaspoons hot sauce
2 teaspoons celery salt
2 tablespoons Worcestershire
  sauce
2 tablespoons soy sauce
2 tablespoons coarsely cut
  horseradish

- Combine all ingredients, stirring well.

Yield: almost 1 gallon

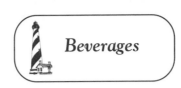

Lemon Tea Punch

12 tea bags
4 teaspoons dried rosemary
2 quarts boiling water
2 cups sugar
2 quarts lemon-lime soda, chilled
1 cup fresh lemon juice, strained
Garnish: fresh lemon slices
Ice ring

- Place tea bags and rosemary in a large saucepan; add 2 quarts boiling water, and steep 5 minutes. Remove and discard tea bags. Add sugar to tea, stirring to dissolve. Strain tea and let cool. Chill until ready to serve.
- Combine tea, soda, and lemon juice in a punch bowl, stirring gently. Garnish, if desired. Float ice ring in tea.

Yield: 30 (½-cup) servings

Classic Eggnog

12 large eggs, separated and at
    room temperature
2 cups sugar
3 tablespoons vanilla extract
2½ cups quality bourbon
⅔ cup quality brandy
4 cups milk
2 cups chilled heavy cream
Freshly grated nutmeg

- Beat yolks at medium speed with an electric mixer until thick and pale. Beat in sugar, 2 tablespoons at a time, beating until thickened. Whisk in vanilla and next 3 ingredients. Pour mixture into a large bowl.
- Beat egg whites in a separate bowl at medium speed until soft peaks form; fold into yolk mixture.
- Beat cream in a separate bowl at medium speed until soft peaks form; fold into yolk mixture. Chill 3 to 5 hours.
- Stir eggnog gently before serving, and sprinkle with nutmeg.

Yield: about 1 quart

Kahlúa

2 cups water
2 ounces instant coffee granules
4 cups white sugar
1 vanilla bean, quartered
1 liter vodka

• Bring 2 cups water to a boil in a saucepan; add coffee granules and sugar, stirring constantly. Return to a boil; boil, stirring constantly, 5 minutes. Remove from heat. Let cool.
• Stir vanilla bean and vodka into coffee mixture and pour into a 1-gallon glass jug. Cover with aluminum foil and screw top on securely. Let age 30 days before using.

Yield: about 1 gallon

JSL Irish Cream

1¾ cups whiskey or rum
1 cup whipping cream
1 (14-ounce) can evaporated milk
3 large eggs
2 tablespoons chocolate syrup
2 teaspoons instant coffee granules
1 teaspoon vanilla extract
½ teaspoon almond extract (or to taste)

• Process all ingredients in a blender until smooth. Chill. Store in the refrigerator up to a month.

This is a wonderful drink for the holidays.

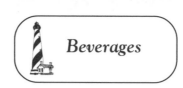

Easy Champagne Punch

1 (16-ounce) can frozen orange
   juice concentrate, undiluted
1 (12-ounce) can frozen
   lemonade concentrate,
   undiluted
1½ cups grenadine syrup
2 (750-ml) bottles champagne
2 (2-liter) bottles ginger ale
Ice ring or ice cubes made from
   lemonade
Garnishes: orange slices, lemon
   slices, maraschino cherries

• Combine first 3 ingredients in a
punch bowl. Gradually add
champagne and ginger ale,
stirring gently to mix. Add ice
ring, and garnish, if desired.
Serve immediately.

Yield: 30 servings

*For a nonalcoholic punch substitute 2 extra bottles ginger ale for cham-
pagne. You can either float the garnishes in the punch bowl or freeze
them in the lemonade ice ring.*

Cranberry Punch

2 cups orange juice
⅓ cup lemon juice
½ cup sugar
1 (48-ounce) bottle cranberry
   juice
2 pints raspberry sherbet
2 (28-ounce) bottles ginger ale,
   chilled

• Combine first 3 ingredients,
stirring until sugar dissolves.
Add cranberry juice, stirring
well. Chill until ready to serve.
• Pour mixture into a punch bowl.
Spoon scoops of sherbet over
top. Add ginger ale, stirring
gently.

Yield: 30 servings

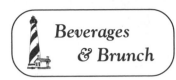

Barney's Slush

2 shots bourbon
6 shots light rum
1 large can peaches, undrained
2 small cans frozen lemonade
   concentrate, undiluted
2 tablespoons powdered sugar

- Process all ingredients in a blender until blended. Add desired amount of crushed ice and process until slushy. Add liquid to slush, if desired, and process to desired consistency. Serve in liqueur glasses with a spoon.

Yield: 6 drinks

Hot Fruit Compote

1 (16-ounce) can peach halves
1 (16-ounce) can pear halves
1 (16-ounce) can pineapple
   chunks
1 (16-ounce) can apricot halves
1 (16-ounce) can pitted dark
   sweet cherries
1 banana, sliced
1 tablespoon lemon juice
12 soft macaroons, crumbled
1 (2-ounce) package sliced
   toasted almonds, divided
¼ cup butter or margarine, cut
   up
⅓ cup amaretto

- Drain canned fruit and combine in a large bowl.
- Combine banana and lemon juice, tossing gently; add to fruit mixture.
- Layer half each of fruit mixture and macaroons in a 2½-quart baking dish. Sprinkle with half of sliced almonds and dot with half of butter. Repeat fruit, macaroon, and butter layers once. Pour amaretto over mixture.
- Bake at 350° for 30 minutes. Sprinkle with remaining half of almonds. Serve warm.

Yield: 16 servings

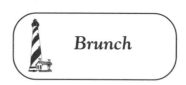
Egg and Sausage Casserole

¼ cup butter or margarine

4 cups unseasoned croutons

2 cups (8 ounces) Cheddar cheese

2 cups milk

8 large eggs, lightly beaten

½ teaspoon dry mustard

12 ounces sausage, cooked, crumbled, and drained

- Place butter in a 7 x 11 x 2-inch baking dish. Place in a 325° oven for 5 minutes or until melted. Tilt dish to coat. Pour croutons over butter and sprinkle with cheese.
- Whisk together milk, eggs, and mustard; pour over cheese. Sprinkle casserole with sausage.
- Bake at 325° for 40 to 50 minutes. Remove from oven and let stand at room temperature 5 to 10 minutes.

Yield: 6 to 8 servings

For a variation, sauté sliced mushrooms, chopped Roma tomato, and sliced small red potatoes in sausage drippings. Sprinkle over top with sausage.

Fluffy Pancakes

1 large egg, lightly beaten

1 cup milk

2 tablespoons vegetable oil

1 cup sifted all-purpose flour

2 tablespoons baking powder

Dash of salt

2 tablespoons sugar

- Whisk together first 3 ingredients.
- Sift together flour and next 3 ingredients; add to egg mixture, beating at medium speed with an electric mixer until smooth.
- Cook spoonfuls of batter on a hot griddle over medium heat until bubbly on 1 side. Turn and cook until done.

Yield: 8 (5-inch) pancakes

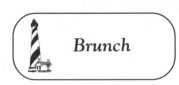

Spinach-Filled Crêpes

1 (10-ounce) package fresh
   spinach, with stems removed
   or 1 (10-ounce) package
   frozen chopped spinach,
   thawed and well drained
2 tablespoons butter or margarine
2 tablespoons all-purpose flour
½ teaspoon salt
½ teaspoon ground nutmeg
Dash of white pepper
½ cup whipping cream
¼ cup (1 ounce) shredded Swiss
   cheese
Crêpes
Grated Parmesan cheese
   (optional)
Garnish: fresh parsley sprigs

• Arrange spinach in a steamer
  basket over boiling water; cover
  and steam 1 to 2 minutes or
  until limp. Drain and rinse in
  cold water. Drain well, pressing
  between layers of paper towels;
  chop.
• Melt butter in a 2-quart
  saucepan over medium heat; stir
  in flour and next 3 ingredient.
  Cook, stirring constantly, 2
  minutes. Gradually stir in cream.
  Cook, stirring constantly, 3
  minutes or until mixture
  thickens. Stir in spinach and
  Swiss cheese.
• Preheat oven to 350°.
• Spoon 1 tablespoon spinach
  mixture into the center of the
  spotty side of 12 crêpes. Roll up
  and arrange in a single layer in a
  baking dish.
• Bake at 350° for 10 minutes or
  until warm. Sprinkle with
  Parmesan cheese, if desired, and
  garnish, if desired.

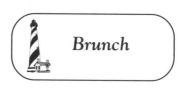

(Spinach-Filled Crêpes continued)

Crêpes

1 cup all-purpose flour
2 tablespoons sugar
1½ cups milk
2 large eggs
1 tablespoon vegetable oil

- Whisk together first 3 ingredients until smooth; add eggs, whisking well. Stir in oil. Chill at least 2 hours.
- Coat bottom of a 6-inch crêpe pan or heavy skillet with vegetable cooking spray; place over medium heat until hot. Pour 2 tablespoons batter into pan; quickly tilt pan in all directions so batter covers bottom of pan. Cook 1 minute or until crêpe can be shaken loose from pan. Turn crêpe, and cook about 30 seconds. Repeat procedure with remaining batter.
- Stack crêpes between sheets of wax paper, and place in an airtight container, if desired. Chill up to 2 days or freeze up to 3 months.

Yield: 12 small crêpes

Spinach-Filled Crêpes can be frozen tightly wrapped in aluminum foil. To serve bake at 350° for 30 minutes or until warm.

Waffles

1½ cups all-purpose flour

1 tablespoon baking powder

¼ teaspoon salt

3 large eggs, separated with egg whites at room temperature

1½ cups milk

⅓ cup butter or margarine, melted

1 tablespoon sugar

- Combine first 3 ingredients in a medium bowl.
- Combine egg yolks, milk, and butter; add to dry ingredients, stirring until mixture is smooth.
- Beat egg whites and sugar at medium speed with an electric mixer until stiff peaks form. Gently fold into flour mixture.
- Pour 1 cup batter into a hot 8-inch waffle iron coated with vegetable cooking spray. Cook 5 minutes or until steaming stops. Repeat procedure with remaining batter.

Yield: 16 (4-inch) waffles

Cheese Grits

1 cup uncooked regular grits

1 stick garlic cheese

½ cup butter or margarine

2 large eggs

½ cup milk

- Cook grits in a medium saucepan according to package directions.
- Melt cheese and butter in a skillet over medium heat, and stir into grits. Whisk together eggs and milk, and stir into grits mixture. Pour into a buttered 7 x 11 x 2-inch baking dish.
- Bake at 350° for 45 minutes.

Yield: 4 to 6 servings

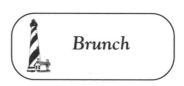
Sugar Nut Sticks

2 cups all-purpose flour
1 tablespoon granulated sugar
¾ cup butter or margarine, cut up
¼ cup milk
1 large egg, lightly beaten
½ cup granulated sugar
¼ cup butter or margarine, softened
½ cup raisins
¼ cup chopped nuts
1 teaspoon almond extract
¼ cup powdered sugar
2 tablespoons water

- Combine flour and 1 tablespoon granulated sugar; cut in ¾ cup butter with a pastry blender until crumbly. Stir in milk and egg until dough forms a ball. Divide into 2 portions. Roll 1 portion into a 12 x 4-inch rectangle on a lightly floured surface. Place on an ungreased baking sheet. Repeat procedure with remaining portion.
- Preheat oven to 350°.
- Combine ½ cup granulated sugar and next 4 ingredients; spread mixture evenly down center of dough rectangles. Bring long edges of dough together, pressing edges to seal.
- Bake at 350° for 30 minutes.
- Combine powdered sugar and 2 tablespoons water, stirring until smooth.
- Remove loaves from the oven; let cool slightly. Drizzle with glaze.

Yield: 2 loaves

Apple Pancakes

3 tablespoons butter or margarine
2 apples, peeled and thinly sliced
½ cup milk
3 large eggs
½ cup all-purpose flour
¼ cup sugar
1 tablespoon ground cinnamon
2 tablespoons butter or
    margarine, melted

• Preheat oven to 450°.
• Melt 3 tablespoons butter in a
  10- to 12-inch ovenproof skillet
  over medium heat; add apple
  and sauté until softened.
• Stir together milk, eggs, and
  flour; pour over apple.
• Combine sugar and cinnamon in
  a small bowl.
• Bake pancake at 450° for
  10 minutes or until puffy and
  browned around the edges.
  Remove from oven, and pour
  melted butter over top. Sprinkle
  with cinnamon mixture. Bake
  5 more minutes or until sugar is
  melted.

Yield: 4 servings

Dr. O's Crab Quiche

½ cup mayonnaise
2 tablespoons all-purpose flour
2 large eggs, lightly beaten
½ cup milk
8 ounces fresh lump crabmeat,
    drained
1½ cups (6 ounces) shredded
    Swiss cheese
⅓ cup chopped green onions
1 partially baked 9-inch pastry
    shell

• Combine first 4 ingredients,
  stirring until well blended; stir in
  crabmeat, cheese, and green
  onions. Pour into pastry shell.
• Bake at 350° for 30 to 40
  minutes or until firm in center.

Yield: 6 to 8 servings

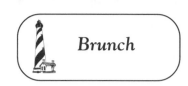

Overnight Caramel French Toast

1 cup firmly packed light brown
  sugar
½ cup butter or margarine
2 tablespoons light corn syrup
12 sandwich bread slices
6 large eggs, lightly beaten
1½ cups milk
1 teaspoon vanilla extract
¼ teaspoon salt

- Cook first 3 ingredients in a small saucepan over medium heat, stirring constantly, until thickened. Pour into a 9 x 13 x 2-inch baking dish. Place 6 bread slices over syrup; top with remaining bread slices.
- Combine eggs and next 3 ingredients, stirring until well blended. Pour evenly over bread slices. Cover and chill 8 hours.
- Bake at 350° for 40 to 45 minutes or until lightly browned.

Yield: 6 to 12 servings

This recipe is really good and very easy. It's great to make the night before and just pop it in the oven in the morning.

Waldorf Whole Wheat Sandwiches

1 (8-ounce) package cream
  cheese, softened
2 teaspoons lemon juice
1 tablespoon milk
1 cup finely chopped apple
½ cup finely chopped pitted dates
½ cup finely chopped walnuts
16 whole wheat bread slices
Butter or margarine, softened

- Stir together first 3 ingredients in a bowl; stir in apple, dates, and walnuts.
- Spread bread slices evenly with butter. Spread ¼ cup apple mixture on each of 8 bread slices. Top with remaining bread.

Yield: 8 sandwiches

Cut these sandwiches into fourths for teas or brunches. The recipe may be halved.

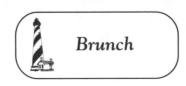
Cranberry-Apple Casserole

½ cup butter or margarine,
  softened
½ cup firmly packed brown sugar
1½ cups uncooked regular
  oatmeal
½ cup chopped pecans
3 cups chopped unpeeled apple
1 pound fresh cranberries
1½ cups sugar
⅓ cup all-purpose flour

- Combine first 4 ingredients in a bowl; set aside.
- Combine apple and next 3 ingredients; spoon into a 3-quart baking dish. Sprinkle pecan mixture over top.
- Bake at 350° for 1 hour.

Yield: 12 servings

This casserole may be made ahead of time. Freeze before baking. To serve, thaw in the refrigerator overnight. Let stand at room temperature 30 minutes before baking. Bake as directed.

Soups & Salads

Bridge of Lions

Begun in 1925 and finished 1927, this has been hailed since its completion as "The Most Beautiful Bridge in Dixie."

It takes its name from the Carrera marble lion statues at its base that were donated by Dr. Andrew Anderson, local physician and philanthropist who believed that St. Augustine needed more works of art in public places. They are copies of the famous lion statues that guard the Loggia dei Lanzi in Florence, Italy.

Originally there were trolley tracks in the south lane of the bridge, and the four tile-roofed towers housed the bridgetender, a tollbooth, and two public restrooms.

The Bridge of Lions is listed on the National Register of Historic Places and is one of the most beloved symbols of the Ancient City.

Soups & Salads

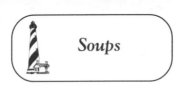

Lentil Soup

1 large onion, chopped
1 celery rib, chopped
1 carrot, chopped
2 to 3 garlic cloves, minced
2 to 4 tablespoons olive oil
1 tomato, seeded and chopped
1 jalapeño pepper, seeded and
    chopped
¼ teaspoon crushed red pepper
1½ teaspoons dried oregano
6 to 8 cups water
4 chicken bouillon cubes
1 (16-ounce) package lentils,
    rinsed
3 ounces dried tomatoes,
    softened in water, drained, and
    chopped
Dash of hot sauce
Salt and ground black pepper to
    taste
Grated Parmesan cheese

- Sauté first 4 ingredients in hot oil in saucepan until tender, stirring constantly. Stir in tomato and next 3 ingredients. Cook, stirring constantly, 15 to 20 minutes or until vegetables are tender.
- Add 6 to 8 cups water, bouillon cubes, and lentils to vegetable mixture. Cover, reduce heat, and simmer 45 minutes or until lentils are tender but not mushy. Stir in dried tomatoes, hot sauce, and salt and pepper to taste.
- Ladle soup into individual bowls, and sprinkle each serving with Parmesan cheese.

Yield: 8 servings

White Chili

2 medium onions, chopped
1 tablespoon olive oil
4 garlic cloves, minced
2 (4.5-ounce) cans chopped
　green chiles
2 teaspoons ground cumin
1½ teaspoons dried oregano
¼ teaspoon ground red pepper
3 to 4 (16-ounce) cans great
　Northern beans, undrained
4 to 6 cups chicken broth
4 cups chopped cooked chicken
　breast
3 cups (12 ounces) shredded
　Monterey Jack cheese
Salt and ground black pepper to
　taste
Sour cream (optional)

- Sauté onion in hot oil in a large
heavy saucepan over medium-
high heat 10 minutes or until
translucent. Stir in garlic and
next 4 ingredients, and cook 2
minutes. Stir in beans and broth;
bring to a boil. Reduce heat, and
stir in chicken and cheese.
Cook, stirring constantly, until
cheese is melted. Season with
salt and pepper to taste.
- Ladle chili into individual bowls.
Top each serving with sour
cream, if desired.

Yield: 8 servings

Tomato Bisque

6 large tomatoes, peeled, seeded,
　and chopped
1 tablespoon chopped fresh basil
¼ cup butter or margarine
3 cups chicken broth
2 cups cream
Salt to taste

- Bring first 4 ingredients to a
simmer in a large saucepan.
Cover and simmer 15 minutes.
Let cool.
- Puree tomato mixture in a
blender until smooth. Return to
saucepan, and stir in cream. Bring
to a simmer, and season with salt
to taste. Serve hot or cold.

Yield: 4 to 6 servings

Vegetarian Chili

1 garlic clove, minced
½ cup chopped onion
1 tablespoon olive oil
¼ cup chopped green onions
¾ cup chopped green bell pepper
1 cup chopped carrot
1 cup chopped celery
1 cup chopped mushrooms
¾ cup chopped pitted ripe olives
2 tablespoons ripe olive juice
1 medium tomato, chopped
1 (4.5-ounce) can chopped green
   chiles
1 (16-ounce) can kidney beans
1 (15-ounce) can tomato sauce
⅓ cup tomato paste
1 (15-ounce) can corn
1 (12-ounce) can beer
½ teaspoon ground cumin
½ teaspoon dried crushed red
   pepper
¼ teaspoon ground red pepper
2 tablespoons chili powder
Salt and ground black pepper to
   taste
1 cup water

• Sauté garlic and ½ cup chopped
onion in hot oil in a large
saucepan 3 to 4 minutes; add
green onions and next 3
ingredients. Cook, stirring
constantly, until vegetables are
tender. Add mushrooms and
next 3 ingredients; cook 5
minutes. Add green chiles and
remaining ingredients, stirring
well. Bring to a boil. Reduce
heat, and simmer 1 to 5 hours.

Yield: 8 servings

The longer you simmer this chili the better the flavors blend.

Cheese Soup

½ cup butter or margarine
½ cup chopped celery
½ cup chopped carrot
¼ cup chopped onion
½ cup all-purpose flour
2 cups chicken broth
1 teaspoon dried thyme
1 bay leaf
6 ounces Brie, with rind removed
½ cup whipping cream

• Melt butter in a saucepan over medium heat; add celery, carrot, and onion, and sauté, stirring constantly, until tender. Add flour, and cook, stirring constantly, 1 minute. Gradually stir in broth, thyme, and bay leaf. Cook, stirring constantly, until mixture is thickened and bubbly. Add cheese, stirring until smooth. Stir in whipping cream, and cook until thoroughly heated. Remove and discard bay leaf.

Yield: 6 servings

Gazpacho

1 large can tomato juice
¼ cup Worcestershire sauce
¼ cup red wine vinegar
1 teaspoon salt
1 cucumber, peeled, seeded, and diced
1 tomato, peeled, seeded, and diced
1 St. Augustine sweet onion, diced
1 large carrot, diced
1 large bell pepper, diced
2 large celery ribs, diced

• Bring first 4 ingredients to a boil in a large Dutch oven over high heat. Turn off heat, and stir in cucumber and remaining ingredients. Chill immediately. Serve cold.

Yield: 6 to 8 servings

Brunswick Stew

1 whole chicken, cut into pieces

1 quart water

2 bacon slices, cut up

1 large onion, sliced

2 carrots, sliced

2 celery ribs, sliced

1 teaspoon salt

1 (28-ounce) can whole tomatoes or 3 large tomatoes, peeled

2 large potatoes, cubed

1 (10-ounce) package frozen butter beans or 1 cup fresh butter beans

½ teaspoon sugar

2 teaspoons salt

½ teaspoon ground black pepper

Dash of ground red pepper

1 tablespoon Worcestershire sauce

1 (16-ounce) package frozen corn kernels or kernels cut from 3 large ears corn

2 tablespoons butter or margarine, melted

2 tablespoons all-purpose flour

- Bring first 7 ingredients to a boil in a 5-quart heavy Dutch oven; reduce heat to medium-low, and cook 2 hours. Remove chicken from broth; let chicken cool. Skin and bone chicken, and cut meat into medium-size pieces. Return to broth.
- Stir tomatoes and next 7 ingredients into broth; cook over medium-low heat, stirring occasionally, 30 minutes. Stir in corn, and cook 30 minutes.
- Combine butter and flour; add to stew, and cook 30 minutes.

Yield: 10 to 12 servings

Butternut Squash Soup

3 to 4 tablespoons unsalted
    butter
3 large leeks, white and light
    green parts sliced
2 pounds butternut squash,
    peeled, seeded, and cubed
4 cups chicken broth
Salt and pepper to taste

- Melt butter in a large Dutch oven over medium heat; add leeks, and sauté until translucent. Add squash and broth, and bring to a boil. Reduce heat, and simmer 30 to 40 minutes or until squash is tender. Remove from heat, and let cool slightly.
- Puree three-fourths of mixture in a food processor or blender until smooth, stopping to scrape down sides. Stir into remaining soup in Dutch oven, and season to taste with salt and pepper.

Yield: 10 servings

Zucchini Bisque

½ cup butter or margarine
1 medium onion, finely chopped
1½ pounds zucchini, cut into
    ¼-inch-thick slices
1 (14½-ounce) can chicken
    broth
1 can water
¼ teaspoon ground nutmeg
½ teaspoon dried basil
1 teaspoon salt
1 pinch ground white pepper
1 cup heavy cream

- Melt butter in a large heavy saucepan over medium heat; add onion, and sauté until tender. Add zucchini, broth, and 1 can water to onion; reduce heat, and simmer 15 minutes.
- Puree half each of zucchini mixture, nutmeg, and next 3 ingredients in a food processor until smooth, stopping to scrape down sides. Repeat procedure once. Combine all of zucchini mixture and cream, stirring until blended.

Yield: 8 servings

Fresh Grouper and Potato Stew

1 cup finely chopped onion

¼ cup olive oil

1 teaspoon finely chopped garlic

1 large tomato, peeled and finely chopped

4 medium-size potatoes, peeled and cut into ¼-inch slices

¼ teaspoon paprika

2 teaspoons salt

¼ teaspoon freshly ground pepper

2 cups boiling water

1 pound fresh grouper, tuna, or halibut, sliced 1 inch thick and cut into 1- x 2-inch pieces

1 cup coarsely crumbled French or Italian bread

- Sauté onion in hot oil in a heavy 3- or 4-quart saucepan until golden; add garlic, and cook 2 minutes. Add tomato, and cook over medium-high heat until most of liquid is evaporated and mixture is thick. Add potato, stirring to coat. Stir in paprika, salt, and pepper. Stir in 2 cups boiling water. Add additional boiling water to cover potato, if necessary. Bring to a boil; cover, reduce heat, and simmer 15 minutes or until potato is barely tender.
- Add fish to stew, and cook, stirring constantly, 5 minutes or until potato is tender and fish flakes easily. Do not overcook.
- Adjust seasonings to taste, and place bread pieces on top. Cover and cook over low heat 3 or 4 minutes. Serve immediately.

Yield: 10 servings

A hearty salad, warm crusty bread, and chilled dry white wine make this meal a memorable one to share with good friends.

Shrimp Chowder

12 ears corn

1½ pounds unpeeled, medium-
   size fresh shrimp

1 pound bacon, cut into strips

1 tablespoon olive oil

3 onions, chopped

5 carrots, sliced diagonally

4 celery ribs, sliced diagonally

1 pound potatoes, peeled and cut
   into ½-inch-thick slices

3¾ cups chicken broth

½ teaspoon dried or 2 teaspoons
   chopped fresh thyme

3 cups milk

1 teaspoon salt

¼ teaspoon pepper

1 teaspoon hot sauce (or to taste)

3 large tomatoes, peeled, seeded,
   and cut into ½-inch cubes

3 tablespoons ½-inch chive
   pieces, divided

- Remove kernels from corn cobs, scraping loose kernels and liquid well and reserving 4 scraped cobs.
- Peel shrimp, and devein, if desired.
- Cook bacon in hot oil in a large skillet until golden but not crisp. Drain well, pressing between layers of paper towels and reserving 2 tablespoons drippings.
- Sauté onion, carrot, and celery in reserved drippings 5 minutes or until tender. Stir in potato, broth, thyme, and reserved 4 cobs broken in half. Cover and simmer until potato is tender. Remove and discard cob halves.
- Stir corn kernels and juice into vegetable mixture. Simmer until corn is tender. Remove 3½ cup solid ingredients; process in a food processor until coarsely chopped, stopping to scrape down sides. Return to remaining chowder. Stir in milk, and simmer until warm. Chill up to 2 days, if desired.
- Stir bacon and shrimp into warm chowder; cover and simmer 3 minutes or until shrimp are opaque. Add salt, pepper, and hot sauce. Stir in tomato and

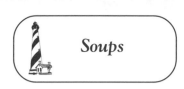
(Shrimp Chowder continued)

half of chives. Simmer until tomato is warm.
- Ladle chowder into individual bowls. Sprinkle servings evenly with remaining chives.

Yield: 16 servings

Pasta e Fagioli

1 pound extra-lean ground beef

1 onion, chopped

2 celery ribs, chopped

2 carrots, shredded

2 (16-ounce) cans Italian-style stewed tomatoes (1 can pureed)

1 (16-ounce) can navy beans

1 (16-ounce) can kidney beans

4 ounces uncooked pasta shells or other small pasta

2 to 4 cans water

Dried oregano to taste

Dried basil to taste

Salt and pepper to taste

Grated Parmesan cheese

- Cook first 4 ingredients in a large Dutch oven over medium heat, stirring until meat crumbles and is no longer pink and vegetables are tender. Add tomatoes and next 7 ingredients; reduce heat, and simmer 30 to 45 minutes or until pasta is tender. Adjust seasonings to taste.
- Spoon soup into individual bowls. Sprinkle each serving with Parmesan cheese.

Yield: 10 servings

This is a hearty Italian favorite with ground beef, white and red beans, tomatoes, and pasta in a savory broth.

Tomato-Florentine Soup

½ cup diced onion

4 garlic cloves, minced

3 to 4 tablespoons olive oil

⅓ cup white wine

1 bay leaf

2 teaspoons celery salt

2 teaspoons dried basil

2 teaspoons dried Italian
  seasoning

1 teaspoon salt

1 teaspoon pepper

2 tablespoons sugar

¼ teaspoon ground nutmeg

1 tablespoon chicken bouillon
  granules

3 tablespoons all-purpose flour

3 cups vegetable juice

2 (28-ounce) cans tomatoes,
  chopped and drained with
  liquid reserved

6 cups milk

1 cup heavy cream

1 (10-ounce) package fresh
  spinach, chopped

3 tablespoons chopped fresh basil

• Sauté onion and garlic in hot oil
  in a large Dutch oven until
  golden; add wine and next
  6 ingredients. Bring to a boil;
  reduce heat, and simmer
  10 minutes. Add sugar, nutmeg,
  and bouillon granules, stirring
  well. Stir in flour.

• Gradually stir vegetable juice
  into onion mixture; cook,
  stirring constantly, over medium
  heat, until smooth. Stir in
  tomatoes and milk; reduce heat,
  and simmer 30 minutes. Stir in
  cream, spinach, and basil;
  simmer 10 to 15 minutes.

Yield: 10 servings

*For a low-fat version, substitute low-fat milk for regular and 1 can
evaporated skimmed milk for cream.*

*Don't let the long list of ingredients deter you from making this soup. It's
delicious!*

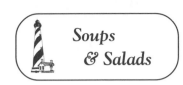
Strawberry-Melon Soup

1 cantaloupe, cubed
1 pint strawberries, hulled
4 cups orange juice, divided
3 tablespoons lemon juice
1 tablespoon strawberry-flavored
   liqueur
¼ teaspoon ground ginger
Garnishes: dollops of sour cream
   or lemon-flavored yogurt,
   fresh mint sprigs

- Process half each cantaloupe and strawberries and ½ cup orange juice in a food processor until smooth, stopping to scrape down sides. Repeat procedure once.
- Combine all of melon mixture, remaining 3½ cups orange juice, and next 3 ingredients, stirring well. Cover and chill.
- Spoon soup into individual bowls. Garnish, if desired.

Yield: 8 to 10 servings

Chicken Salad

2 bone-in chicken breasts
   (2½ pounds)
Salt and pepper to taste
1¼ cups mayonnaise
1 cup fresh basil, finely chopped
2 to 3 garlic cloves, chopped
3 tablespoons sunflower seeds or
   pine nuts
4 celery ribs, chopped
⅔ cup freshly grated Parmesan
   cheese

- Sprinkle chicken breasts with salt and pepper. Bake at 375° for 1 hour or until done. Let cool. Skin and bone chicken; chop meat.
- Process mayonnaise and next 3 ingredients in a food processor until smooth, stopping to scrape down sides.
- Combine chicken, mayonnaise mixture, celery, and Parmesan cheese. Serve as a sandwich or on lettuce-lined plates.

Yield: 6 to 8 servings

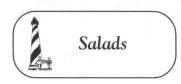

Strawberry-Spinach Salad

½ cup sugar

½ cup vegetable oil

¼ cup apple cider vinegar

¼ teaspoon Worcestershire sauce

¼ teaspoon paprika

2 teaspoons poppy seeds

1 (10-ounce) package fresh spinach

½ pint strawberries, sliced

¼ to ½ cup crushed peanut brittle

• Whisk together first 6 ingredients.
• Sprinkle strawberries and peanut brittle over spinach; serve with dressing.

Yield: 6 servings

Hot Seafood Salad

1 (6-ounce) can crabmeat, drained

1 (6-ounce) can shrimp, drained

1 cup mayonnaise

1 green bell pepper, chopped

1 small onion, chopped

½ teaspoon salt

1 teaspoon Worcestershire sauce

1 cup celery, chopped

1 cup buttered breadcrumbs

• Combine first 8 ingredients, stirring well. Spoon into a 2-quart baking dish. Sprinkle with breadcrumbs.
• Bake at 350° for 30 minutes.

Yield: 4 servings

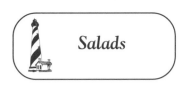

Rice Salad with Artichoke Hearts

1 (8-ounce) package yellow rice
1 (6-ounce) jar marinated
    artichoke hearts, drained with
    liquid reserved
⅓ cup chopped green bell pepper
4 green onions, chopped
8 pimiento-stuffed olives, sliced
⅔ cup mayonnaise
1 teaspoon curry powder

• Prepare rice according to
package directions, omitting
butter. Combine rice mixture,
artichoke hearts, and next 3
ingredients in a serving bowl.
• Combine artichoke liquid,
mayonnaise, and curry powder;
pour over salad. Chill.

Yield: 6 to 8 servings

You can also add chopped cooked chicken to this salad.

Dutch Treat Cole Slaw

6 to 8 cups shredded cabbage
1 cup shredded carrot
½ cup chopped green bell pepper
⅓ cup sugar
½ teaspoon unflavored gelatin
¼ cup cider vinegar
2 tablespoons cold water
⅓ cup canola oil
1 teaspoon celery seeds
⅛ teaspoon salt
⅛ teaspoon pepper
¼ cup sour cream

• Toss together first 3 ingredients
in a large bowl.
• Stir together sugar and gelatin in
a small saucepan; add vinegar
and 2 tablespoons cold water.
Bring to a boil, stirring
constantly. Remove from heat,
and let cool.
• Process dressing, oil, and next
3 ingredients in a blender until
well blended. Add sour cream,
blending just until combined.
Pour over vegetables, tossing to
coat. Cover and chill several
hours.

Yield: 10 to 12 servings

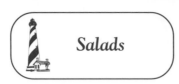

Fourth of July Summer Salad

4 cups boiling water, divided

1 (6-ounce) package strawberry-flavored gelatin

1 (10-ounce) package frozen strawberries, unthawed

1 (8-ounce) package cream cheese, softened

1 (8-ounce) container sour cream

¾ cup mayonnaise

1 tablespoon lemon juice

1 envelope unflavored gelatin

¾ cup cold water, divided

1 (6-ounce) package blackberry-flavored gelatin

2 cups frozen blueberries

- Pour 2 cups boiling water over strawberry gelatin, stirring until dissolved. Gently stir in strawberries. Chill until mixture begins to thicken. Stir to distribute berries evenly; turn into a lightly oiled 11- to 12-cup mold. Chill.
- Beat cream cheese and next 3 ingredients at medium speed with an electric mixer until smooth.
- Sprinkle unflavored gelatin over ¼ cup cold water in a small custard cup. Heat over boiling water in a ½-inch water bath, stirring until dissolved. Add to cream cheese mixture, beating until well blended. Gently spoon over strawberry mixture, spreading evenly to edges. Chill.
- Pour remaining 2 cups boiling water over blackberry gelatin, stirring until dissolved. Gently stir in remaining ½ cup cold water and blackberries. Chill until mixture begins to thicken. Stir to distribute berries evenly; spoon over cream cheese layer, spreading evenly to edges. Chill overnight or until firm.
- Loosen edges with the tip of a sharp knife; dip the mold into warm water to the depth of the gelatin for 5 seconds. Tilt or shake mold gently to loosen.

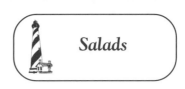
(Fourth of July Summer Salad continued)

Invert a serving plate over mold; hold both firmly together, and invert, shaking mold gently until gelatin slips onto plate. Repeat procedure if gelatin will not release.

Yield: 12 servings

Summer Rice Salad

⅔ cup uncooked long-grain rice

1½ cups water

¼ teaspoon salt

2 tablespoons chopped fresh parsley

2 tablespoons chopped fresh dill

1 teaspoon grated lemon rind

2 tablespoons fresh lemon juice

2 tablespoons water

2 tablespoons olive oil

1 teaspoon Dijon mustard

⅛ teaspoon pepper

1 cup finely chopped yellow squash

1 cup small broccoli florets, blanched and cooled

3 radishes, thinly sliced

1 green onion, thinly sliced

- Bring first 3 ingredients to a boil in a small saucepan; cover, reduce heat, and simmer 20 minutes or until water is absorbed. Rinse with cold water, and drain.
- Whisk together parsley and next 7 ingredients in a large bowl. Add rice and vegetables, tossing to coat. Cover and chill 6 to 24 hours, stirring occasionally. Serve cold.

Yield: 6 servings

Chopped red bell pepper or cherry tomato halves may be substituted for radishes, if desired.

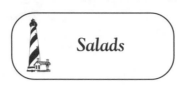

Cider Mill Spinach Salad

¾ cup crumbled blue cheese, divided

1 pound fresh spinach, stemmed and torn into bite-size pieces

2 apples, finely chopped

½ cup chopped walnuts

1 cup mayonnaise

½ cup sour cream

⅛ teaspoon salt

⅛ teaspoon pepper

6 bacon slices, cooked and crumbled

- Toss together ½ cup blue cheese and next 3 ingredients in a serving bowl. Chill until ready to serve.
- Combine remaining ¼ cup blue cheese, mayonnaise, and next 3 ingredients, stirring well. Cover and chill until ready to serve.
- Pour dressing over spinach mixture, tossing gently. Sprinkle with bacon, and serve immediately.

Yield: 6 to 8 servings

Triplet Salad

2 tablespoons olive oil

2 tablespoons red wine or balsamic vinegar

1 to 4 garlic cloves, minced

⅛ teaspoon salt

2 cups romaine lettuce, torn

2 cups leaf lettuce, torn

2 cups Boston lettuce, torn

1 (11-ounce) can mandarin oranges, drained

1 cup seedless red grapes, halved

½ cup thinly sliced purple onion

⅓ cup toasted slivered almonds

- Combine first 4 ingredients in a jar; cover tightly, and shake vigorously. Chill until ready to serve.
- Combine romaine lettuce and next 5 ingredients in a large serving bowl. Pour dressing over salad, tossing to coat. Sprinkle with almonds.

Yield: 6 servings

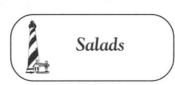
Seafood Pasta Salad

8 ounces pasta shells, cooked
8 ounces imitation crab chunks
8 ounces imitation lobster
   chunks
1 cup chopped celery
1 cup chopped green onions
½ cup chopped green bell pepper
¼ cup finely chopped parsley
1 cup mayonnaise
1 cup sour cream
½ cup Dat'l Do-It sauce
¼ cup Dijon mustard

- Combine first 7 ingredients in a large bowl.
- Combine mayonnaise and next 3 ingredients, stirring well. Pour over seafood mixture, tossing to coat. Chill up to 24 hours.

Yield: 8 servings

Artichoke-Rice Salad

2 cups chicken broth
1 cup uncooked rice
½ cup chopped green onions
¼ cup chopped green bell pepper
½ cup sliced pimiento-stuffed
   olives
1 (6-ounce) jar marinated
   artichoke hearts, halved
½ cup mayonnaise
½ teaspoon dried dill weed
½ teaspoon salt
Garnish: pimiento-stuffed olives

- Bring broth to a boil in a saucepan, and add rice. Cover and cook 20 minutes. Chill.
- Combine chilled rice, green onions, and next 6 ingredients, stirring well. Garnish, if desired.

Yield: 6 to 8 servings

24-Hour Salad

2 large eggs, lightly beaten

2 tablespoons sugar

2 tablespoons orange juice

2 tablespoons vinegar

1 tablespoon butter or margarine

½ teaspoon salt

1 (16-ounce) container sour cream

1 cup seedless grapes, halved

1 cup dried banana slices

1 (15¼-ounce) can pineapple tidbits, drained

1 cup pitted Bing cherries

1 cup finely chopped orange

1 cup cantaloupe balls

2 plums, sliced

2 cups miniature marshmallows

Lettuce leaves

- Cook first 4 ingredients in a small saucepan over medium heat, stirring constantly, just until thickened. Immediately remove from heat; stir in butter and salt. Let cool.
- Place sour cream in a medium bowl; gently fold in egg mixture. Cover and chill.
- Combine grapes and next 7 ingredients in a large bowl; pour chilled dressing over top, stirring to coat. Cover and chill overnight.
- Serve salad on individual lettuce-lined plates.

Yield: 16 servings

Watch the dressing carefully, if it cooks too long the eggs will curdle.

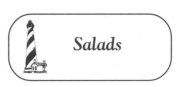
Sweet Potato Salad

3 pounds sweet potatoes, peeled
   and cubed

⅛ teaspoon salt

1½ cups sour cream

⅔ cup mayonnaise

2 tablespoons chopped
   crystallized ginger

2 teaspoons grated orange rind

1 (20-ounce) can crushed
   pineapple, well drained

4 to 5 celery ribs, sliced with
   leaves reserved

1 cup walnut halves

1 cup raisins

• Bring sweet potato, salt, and
  water to cover to a boil in a large
  saucepan; reduce heat, and
  simmer 10 to 15 minutes or just
  until tender. Drain and let cool.
• Beat sour cream and next 3
  ingredients at medium speed
  with an electric mixer until
  creamy.
• Combine sweet potato,
  pineapple, and next 3
  ingredients in a large bowl,
  stirring gently. Gradually add
  mayonnaise mixture, tossing
  gently. Cover and chill 12 to 24
  hours. Serve cold. Garnish with
  celery leaves.

Yield: 12 servings

This easy salad is a nice alternative to traditional potato salad.
It's very pretty if the potatoes don't get too mashed.

Four Bean Salad

1 medium-size green bell pepper,
   thinly sliced into rings

1 medium onion, thinly sliced
   and separated into rings

1 (16-ounce) can green beans,
   drained

1 (15-ounce) can cut yellow wax
   beans, rinsed and drained

1 (15½-ounce) can garbanzo
   beans, rinsed and drained

1 (15½-ounce) can red kidney
   beans, rinsed and drained

½ cup white wine vinegar

⅓ cup vegetable oil

¼ cup sugar

2 tablespoons chopped fresh
   parsley

1 teaspoon dried basil, crushed

½ teaspoon dried tarragon,
   crushed

¼ teaspoon salt

1 teaspoon dry mustard

1 head romaine lettuce, separated
   into leaves and stemmed

- Cut onion and bell pepper rings
  in half, reserving several rings
  for garnish. Stir together onion
  and bell pepper ring halves,
  green beans, and next
  3 ingredients in a large bowl.
- Combine vinegar and next
  7 ingredients in a jar; cover
  tightly, and shake vigorously.
  Drizzle dressing over bean
  mixture. Cover and chill at least
  3 hours, stirring twice.
- Stir bean mixture, and drain.
  Spoon into a lettuce-lined salad
  bowl. Garnish with reserved
  onion and bell pepper rings.

Yield: 8 to 10 servings

*This is a great make-ahead salad that's especially good if left overnight.
You can use different types of beans and lettuce, if desired. It's also
really good with corn.*

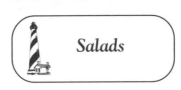
Chilled Lemony Mushrooms

3 pounds medium-size fresh
   mushrooms,

3 lemons

¾ cup vegetable oil

6 tablespoons water

4½ teaspoons soy sauce

¾ teaspoon salt

¾ teaspoon sugar

¾ teaspoon rubbed sage

6 small heads Bibb lettuce

24 cherry tomatoes, halved

- Trim tough stem ends, and slice mushrooms.
- Cut 18 thin lemon slices, and squeeze 6 teaspoons fresh lemon juice.
- Cook mushroom slices in hot oil in a large saucepan over medium-high heat, stirring frequently, until well coated. Stir in lemon slices, juice, 6 tablespoons water, and next 4 ingredients; bring to a boil. Reduce heat to medium, and cook, stirring often, 3 minutes or until mushrooms are tender. Transfer mixture to a glass or plastic bowl; cover and chill.
- Cut each head of lettuce into 4 wedges. Arrange mushrooms and lettuce on 24 salad plates. Place 2 cherry tomato halves on each plate. Serve immediately.

Yield: 24 servings

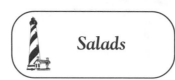
Zucchini Salad with Poppy Seed Vinaigrette

2 tablespoons balsamic or red
   wine vinegar

2 tablespoons orange or lemon
   juice

1 tablespoon poppy seeds

1 teaspoon sugar

½ teaspoon dry mustard

¼ teaspoon salt

⅓ cup canola oil

1 green onion, minced

8 large zucchini, halved
   lengthwise and thinly sliced
   crosswise

• Whisk together first 6
  ingredients in a large bowl;
  gradually whisk in oil. Stir in
  green onion. Cover and chill.

• Place zucchini in a large bowl;
  whisk vinaigrette, and pour
  desired amount over zucchini.

Yield: 6 cups

Vinaigrette can be made a day ahead. Orange juice will give the vinaigrette a sweet flavor; lemon juice will give it a tart flavor.

Broccoli-Raisin Salad

1 head broccoli

1 pound bacon, cooked and
   crumbled

1 cup raisins

1 medium-size purple onion,
   chopped

1 cup mayonnaise

2 teaspoons vinegar

2 teaspoons sugar

• Remove and discard broccoli
  stalks; chop florets into bite-size
  pieces. Combine broccoli and
  remaining ingredients, stirring
  well. Chill at least 6 hours.

Yield: 8 to 10 servings

This salad is best if made a day ahead .

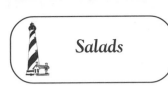

Tabbouleh

½ cup burghul (cracked wheat)

¼ cup chopped fresh or
2 teaspoons dried mint, finely
chopped

2 bunches fresh parsley,
stemmed and chopped

3 medium tomatoes, diced

1 bunch green onions, finely
chopped

Juice of 2 lemons

¼ cup olive oil

1¼ teaspoons salt

½ teaspoon pepper

Dash of ground allspice

• Soak burghul in water to cover
at least 30 minutes. Squeeze out
moisture, and transfer to a large
bowl. Add mint and next 3
ingredients, tossing gently. Add
lemon juice and next 4
ingredients, stirring well. Cover
and chill at least 1 hour.

Yield: 8 servings

Green Salad with Warm Brie Dressing

2 tablespoons chopped walnuts

1 cup torn Boston lettuce

1 cup torn romaine lettuce

⅓ cup low-fat Italian dressing

1 ounce Brie cheese, with rind
removed

• Bake walnuts on an ungreased
baking sheet at 350°, stirring
twice, 10 to 15 minutes or until
toasted.
• Toss together lettuces, and place
on 4 individual plates.
• Microwave dressing at HIGH 30
seconds; add Brie, stirring until
melted. Spoon dressing evenly
over lettuce, and sprinkle with
toasted walnuts.

Yield: 4 servings

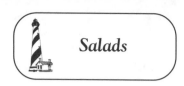

Sesame Seed Dressing

2 tablespoons sesame seeds
2 tablespoons sugar
¼ teaspoon paprika
⅛ teaspoon salt
¼ teaspoon Worcestershire sauce
⅛ teaspoon dry mustard
½ cup vegetable oil
¼ cup cider vinegar
1 teaspoon grated onion

- Bake sesame seeds in a thin layer on a baking sheet at 350°, stirring 3 times, 10 to 15 minutes or until golden brown.
- Combine sugar and next 4 ingredients in a small bowl; beat mixture at medium speed with an electric mixer adding oil and vinegar alternately. Stir in onion and sesame seeds. Cover tightly, and chill. Shake well before serving. Serve over prepared vegetables.

Yield: 2 cups

To use dressing with fruit, increase sugar to 4 tablespoons.

Tangy Sunshine Dressing

¼ cup orange juice
¼ cup honey
2 tablespoons cider vinegar
⅛ teaspoon salt
⅛ teaspoon ground cinnamon
⅔ cup vegetable oil
1 tablespoon poppy seeds

- Combine first 5 ingredients in a small bowl; beat mixture at medium speed with an electric mixer gradually adding oil. Stir in poppy seeds. Cover tightly, and chill up to 2 weeks. Toss dressing with fresh cut fruit.

Yield: 1⅓ cups

Any vinegar may be substituted for cider vinegar; the dressing flavor will change slightly. Store poppy seeds in an airtight container in the refrigerator or freezer because they go bad quickly.

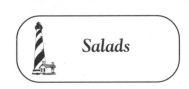

Buttermilk and Blue Cheese Dressing

½ cup mayonnaise

¼ cup buttermilk

1 tablespoon lemon juice

1 tablespoon chopped fresh
  parsley

½ teaspoon minced garlic

4 ounces blue cheese, finely
  crumbled

• Beat first 5 ingredients at
medium speed with an electric
mixer until blended; stir in blue
cheese. Cover tightly, and chill
at least overnight and up to 1
week. Serve on salad, as a dip for
vegetables, or as a sandwich or
burger spread.

Yield: 1¼ cups

*For a low-fat version, substitute reduced-fat mayonnaise for regular and
decrease blue cheese to 2 ounces. Feta may be substituted for blue cheese
for a milder flavor.*

Hot Chicken Salad

4 cups chopped cooked chicken,
  chilled

4 hard-cooked eggs, chopped

1 (10¾-ounce) can cream of
  chicken or celery soup,
  undiluted

1 cup chopped celery

¾ cup mayonnaise or dressing

2 pimientos, chopped

2 tablespoons lemon juice

1 teaspoon finely chopped onion

1 cup (4 ounces) shredded
  Cheddar cheese

1½ cups crushed potato chips

⅔ cup slivered almonds

• Stir together first 8 ingredients;
spoon into a greased 2-quart
baking dish. Sprinkle with
cheese.

• Combine potato chips and
almonds in a small bowl;
sprinkle over casserole. Cover
and chill overnight.

• Preheat oven to 400°.

• Bake at 400° for 30 minutes or
until thoroughly heated,
covering with aluminum foil to
prevent over browning, if
necessary.

Yield: 8 servings

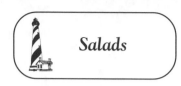
Jane's Italian Pasta Salad

8 ounces rotini pasta, cooked

1 medium zucchini, sliced
(1¼ cups)

1 medium-size green bell pepper,
chopped (¾ cup)

1 medium-size red or yellow bell
pepper, chopped (¾ cup)

1 tomato, seeded and chopped
(⅔ cup)

3 ounces sliced pepperoni

2 ounces provolone cheese,
cubed

½ cup chopped fresh parsley

¼ cup chopped purple onion

15 pitted ripe olives

Vinaigrette

Garnish: fresh basil sprigs

Vinaigrette

¼ cup balsamic vinegar

1 garlic clove, minced

2 tablespoons vegetable oil

2 tablespoons olive oil

1 teaspoon dried basil

¼ teaspoon salt

¼ teaspoon dried oregano

¼ teaspoon freshly ground
pepper

• Combine first 10 ingredients in a
large bowl, tossing well. Pour
Vinaigrette over salad, tossing to
coat. Chill overnight, if desired.
Let stand at room temperature
30 minutes before serving.
Garnish, if desired.

• Combine all ingredients in a jar;
cover tightly, and shake
vigorously.

Yield: 8 to 10 servings

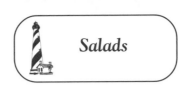
Sunshine Snow Pea Salad

¼ cup sesame seeds
½ cup vegetable oil
2 tablespoons lemon juice
2 tablespoons vinegar
2 tablespoons sugar
1 garlic clove, crushed
1 pound fresh snow pea pods, stemmed
4 bacon slices, cooked and crumbled
4 cups shredded lettuce
½ cup chopped fresh parsley
Carrots, thinly sliced

- Bake sesame seeds in a thin layer on a baking sheet at 350°, stirring 3 times, 10 to 15 minutes or until golden brown. Combine toasted sesame seeds and next 5 ingredients in a jar; cover tightly, and shake vigorously. Chill.
- Arrange pea pods in a steamer basket over boiling water; cover and steam 30 seconds. Remove from steamer basket; cover and chill up to 3 days.
- Toss together pea pods, bacon, lettuce, and parsley in a large salad bowl. Shake dressing, and pour desired amount over salad, tossing to coat. Top with carrot.

Yield: 8 servings

The dressing is also very good for spinach salad. Cut the carrot into flower shapes using a canapé cutter for a decorative touch.

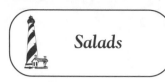
C.W.'s Cobb Salad

8 cups torn iceberg lettuce

2½ cups torn chicory, escarole, or radicchio

1½ cups torn watercress

1¾ cups chopped tomato

2½ cups cubed cooked chicken breast

6 bacon slices, cooked and crumbled

2 hard-cooked eggs, diced

⅔ cup crumbled blue cheese

2 cups diced green bell pepper and/or avocado

C.W.'s Dressing

2 tablespoons chopped fresh chives

C.W.'s Dressing

⅔ cup vegetable oil

⅓ cup white wine vinegar

1 garlic clove, halved

½ teaspoon Worcestershire sauce

½ teaspoon dry mustard

½ teaspoon paprika

½ teaspoon sugar

¼ teaspoon pepper

• Toss together first 3 ingredients; line a large platter or shallow bowl with greens. Arrange tomato and next 5 ingredients over greens.
• Shake dressing well; remove and discard garlic.
• Present arranged salad to your guests. Pour desired amount of dressing over salad, tossing to coat. Sprinkle with chives, and serve.

• Combine all ingredients in a jar; cover tightly, and shake vigorously.

Yield: 6 servings

Entrées

Ponce de Leon Hotel

Begun in 1885, completed in 1887, and opened in 1888, this hotel marked Henry Flagler's entrance into Florida in a grand way.

Architects John Carrere and Thomas Hastings designed the hotel not to overwhelm St. Augustine, but to blend in with it, a task at which they succeeded admirably.

Guests over the years included Mark Twain, Theodore Roosevelt, Babe Ruth, John L. Lewis and Katharine Hepburn.

The hotel's longtime head-waiter, Frank P. Thompson, organized the first black professional baseball team, the Cuban Giants, in the 1880s.

It closed as a hotel in the 1960s and entered its second life as a school, Flagler College.

It is listed on the National Register of Historic Places and is recognized as one of the most extraordinary buildings in the United States.

Entrées

Beef

Venison

Lamb

Pork

Poultry

Casseroles

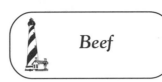

Osso Buco

3 fresh parsley sprigs

1 fresh thyme sprig

1 bay leaf

8 (2-inch-thick) veal shanks

½ teaspoon salt

1 teaspoon pepper

¼ cup olive oil, divided

2 large onions, chopped

3 large carrots, cut into ½-inch cubes

3 celery ribs, cut into ½-inch cubes

2 cups dry white wine

4 cups hot water

4 teaspoons beef bouillon granules

1 tablespoon all-purpose flour

1 tablespoon butter or margarine, softened

- Tie together first 3 ingredients with kitchen string; set aside.
- Rub veal with salt and pepper.
- Brown half of veal in 1½ tablespoons hot oil in a large skillet over medium-high heat turning often 5 minutes. Remove to a roasting pan; keep warm. Repeat with 1½ tablespoons oil and remaining veal.
- Sauté onion, carrot, and celery in remaining 1 tablespoon hot oil in skillet until tender. Add wine; bring to a boil and boil, stirring occasionally, until reduced by two-thirds (about 15 minutes). Add 4 cups hot water, bouillon, and herb bundle; cover and bring to a boil. Pour over veal.
- Bake covered, at 375° for 1 hour and 45 minutes or until veal is tender.
- Remove veal from pan; keep warm. Pour drippings through a wire-mesh strainer into a skillet, discarding solids. Bring to a boil and boil until reduced by half (about 40 minutes).
- Whisk together flour and butter until smooth; whisk into drippings. Cook, whisking constantly, 1 minute or until thickened. Serve with veal.

Yield: 8 servings

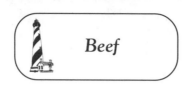
Mushroom-Stuffed Beef Tenderloin

1¼ cups Marsala wine, divided

¼ cup minced onion

¼ cup olive oil

2 tablespoons red wine vinegar

½ teaspoon salt

½ teaspoon pepper

1 (5- to 6-pound) beef
    tenderloin, trimmed

3 tablespoons butter or margarine

1 pound fresh mushrooms, sliced

⅓ cup sliced green onions

2 garlic cloves, crushed

1½ cups soft whole wheat
    breadcrumbs

Garlic salt to taste

Freshly ground pepper to taste

8 bacon slices

Garnishes: tomato roses, fresh
    parsley sprigs

• Stir together ¾ cup wine and
next 5 ingredients. Place
tenderloin in a large shallow
dish; pour wine mixture over
top. Cover and chill 8 hours,
turning occasionally.

• Melt butter in a skillet over
medium heat; add mushrooms,
green onions, and garlic, and
sauté until tender. Add
remaining ½ cup wine and
simmer until liquid is absorbed.
Remove from heat and add
breadcrumbs, tossing gently.

• Remove tenderloin from
marinade, discarding marinade.
Slice tenderloin lengthwise to
but not through the center,
leaving 1 long side connected.

• Spoon stuffing mixture into
tenderloin opening; fold top side
over stuffing, and tie securely
with heavy string at 2-inch
intervals. Sprinkle with garlic
salt and pepper to taste. Place
tenderloin, seam side down, on a
rack in a roasting pan.

• Bake at 425° for 30 minutes. Cut
and remove strings from
tenderloin. Arrange bacon slices
in a crisscross pattern over
tenderloin, securing at ends with
wooden picks. Bake 15 to
20 more minutes or until bacon
is crisp and a meat thermometer

(Mushroom-Stuffed Beef Tenderloin continued)

inserted into thickest portion registers 140° (rare). (Bake until thermometer registers 150° for medium rare or 160° for medium.) Remove and discard wooden picks. Garnish, if desired.

Yield: 10 to 12 servings

Lite Mexican Meat Loaf

½ cup chopped onion

½ cup chopped green bell pepper

⅓ cup chopped fresh cilantro

2 tablespoons minced seeded jalapeño pepper

1 teaspoon salt

2 teaspoons ground cumin

2 teaspoons chili powder

¼ teaspoon pepper

4 taco shells, crushed (about 1½ ounces)

2 egg whites

3 garlic cloves, minced

1 (15-ounce) can black beans, rinsed and drained

2 pounds ground round

• Preheat oven to 375°.
• Stir together first 12 ingredients in a large bowl. Crumble meat over vegetable mixture, stirring just until blended. Press meat mixture into a 9 x 5-inch loaf pan coated with vegetable cooking spray.
• Bake at 375° for 1 hour or until a meat thermometer inserted into loaf registers 160°. Remove from oven, and let stand 10 minutes.
• Remove meat loaf from pan and cut into 16 slices. Serve with salsa, if desired.

Yield: 8 servings

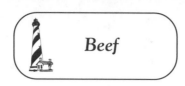

Dorothy's Flank Steak

3 pounds flank steak
¼ cup sesame seeds
½ cup vegetable oil
½ cup soy sauce
1 cup finely chopped onion
½ teaspoon pepper
½ teaspoon ground ginger
4 teaspoons brown sugar

- Combine all ingredients in a heavy-duty zip-top plastic bag; seal and turn to coat. Chill 2 hours or overnight.
- Remove steak from marinade, discarding marinade. Grill steak over medium heat (300° to 350°) 4 to 6 minutes on each side (for rare to medium rare).

Yield: 6 to 8 servings

Art's Prime Rib

1 (4- to 5-pound) standing rib roast
½ cup Worcestershire sauce
1 tablespoon liquid from hot peppers in vinegar
1 (1-ounce) envelope dry onion soup mix

- Combine all ingredients in a heavy-duty zip-top plastic bag; seal and turn to coat. Chill overnight.
- Prepare a charcoal fire in grill 2½ hours before dinner, keeping charcoal all to 1 side (do not spread out). Let burn 15 minutes. Remove meat from marinade, discarding marinade. Grill meat, bone side down and covered with grill lid, 2 hours (rare to medium rare). (Add 15 minutes for desired degrees of doneness.)

Yield: 6 servings

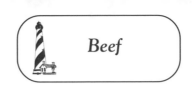

Beef Burgundy

3 pounds stew beef, cut into bite-size pieces

1 (10¾-ounce) can cream of mushroom soup, undiluted

1 (1-ounce) envelope dry onion soup mix

1 cup Burgundy

1 (8-ounce) package fresh mushrooms, sliced

Hot cooked egg noodles

Poppy seeds to taste

• Combine first 4 ingredients in a large roasting pan.
• Bake at 350° for 2½ hours; stir in mushrooms and bake 30 more minutes. Serve over hot cooked egg noodles and sprinkle with poppy seeds to taste.

Yield: 6 servings

Green Peppercorn Cream Sauce

6 tablespoons butter or margarine

2 tablespoons minced shallots

1 pinch all-purpose flour

1 cup heavy cream

4 tablespoons brandy

Salt and pepper to taste

1 tablespoons drained green peppercorns

• Melt butter in a skillet over medium heat; add shallots and sauté 2 minutes. Stir in flour. Stir in cream and cook until slightly thickened (do not boil). Stir in brandy and cook 2 minutes. Season with salt and pepper to taste. Stir in peppercorns.

Yield: 1¼ cups

Serve this sauce over chicken breasts, steak, or pasta.

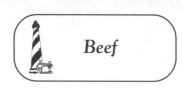

Marinated Tenderloin with Horseradish Sauce

1 (5- to 8-pound) tenderloin
Lemon pepper
2 garlic cloves, crushed
2 cups soy sauce
½ cup cognac
Horseradish Sauce

Horseradish Sauce
1 cup sour cream
½ cup firmly packed fresh
   parsley leaves
3 tablespoons prepared
   horseradish
5 teaspoons lemon juice
1 teaspoon salt
½ cup heavy cream, whipped

- Combine first 5 ingredients in a heavy-duty zip-top plastic bag; chill 4 hours. Remove from refrigerator and bring to room temperature.
- Preheat oven to 500°.
- Remove roast from marinade, discarding marinade; place in a roasting pan. Place roast in oven and reduce oven temperature to 350°. Bake 45 minutes or until a meat thermometer inserted into thickest portion registers 135°.
- Slice roast, and serve warm or at room temperature with Horseradish Sauce and rolls.

- Puree first 5 ingredients in a food processor until smooth, stopping to scrape down sides. Fold in heavy cream. Chill 4 hours.

Yield: 10 to 12 servings

Bourbon BBQ Sauce

1 cup butter or margarine
1 medium onion, chopped
1 teaspoon garlic salt
3 tablespoons vinegar
1 tablespoon salt
½ cup firmly packed brown sugar
¾ cup prepared mustard
1 tablespoon pepper
¼ cup bourbon

• Melt butter in a skillet over medium heat; add onion, and sauté until tender. Stir in garlic salt and next 5 ingredients and cook 5 minutes. Remove from heat and stir in bourbon. Store in a glass container in the refrigerator.

Beans and Venison

2 cups dried red kidney beans
1 to 2 pounds venison, cut into chunks
1 large onion, chopped
Salt pork
¼ cup sugar
Salt and pepper to taste

• Wash beans and cover with 3 to 4 times as much water as beans in a large Dutch oven. Remove beans that float. Bring beans to a boil; reduce heat and simmer a few minutes. Remove from heat, and let stand at room temperature 10 minutes. Add venison and next 4 ingredients.
• Bake at 350° for 4 hours or until venison is tender.

Yield: 8 servings

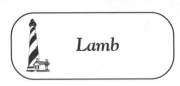

Lamb Chops with Mint Pesto

8 lamb rib chops
2 garlic cloves, minced
½ teaspoon salt
½ teaspoon pepper
2 tablespoons minced fresh or
   2 teaspoons dried mint
2 tablespoons olive oil
Mint Pesto

Mint Pesto
2 cups loosely packed fresh mint
   leaves
½ cup loosely packed fresh
   parsley leaves
2 garlic cloves
¼ cup extra-virgin olive oil
¼ teaspoon salt
⅛ teaspoon pepper
½ cup grated Parmesan cheese
¼ cup pine nuts, toasted
1 tablespoon lemon juice

- Place lamb chops in a large baking dish; sprinkle with garlic and next 4 ingredients. Cover and chill at least 6 hours.
- Grill chops over medium heat (300° to 350°) 3 to 4 minutes on each side (for medium rare) or until well browned. Serve chops with Mint Pesto.

- Process all ingredients in a food processor until a coarse paste forms, stopping to scrape down sides.

Yield: 8 servings

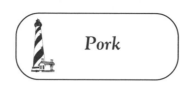
Pork au Poivre

⅓ cup Dijon mustard
¼ cup olive oil
1 tablespoon dried tarragon
1 teaspoon pepper
1 (1½-pound) pork tenderloin,
  sliced

- Combine all ingredients in a
  heavy-duty zip-top plastic bag;
  seal and turn to coat. Chill
  2 hours. Remove pork from
  marinade, reserving marinade.
- Sauté pork in a skillet over
  medium heat 3 to 4 minutes on
  each side, basting with reserved
  marinade.

Yield: 6 servings

Italian Sausage with Red Sauce

1 pound hot Italian sausage
2 tablespoons olive oil, divided
1 large onion, chopped
1 (8-ounce) package fresh
  mushrooms, sliced
½ green bell pepper, chopped
1 garlic clove, minced
¼ cup white wine
1 (15-ounce) can tomato sauce
1 (14½-ounce) can stewed
  tomatoes, drained
½ teaspoon dried Italian
  seasoning
Hot cooked pasta

- Brown sausage in 1 tablespoon
  hot oil in a skillet over medium
  heat, turning occasionally.
  Remove from skillet.
- Sauté onion in remaining 1
  tablespoon hot oil in skillet 5
  minutes; add mushrooms, bell
  pepper, and garlic, and cook 5
  minutes. Stir in wine, and cook
  2 minutes. Stir in tomato sauce,
  stewed tomatoes, and Italian
  seasoning; bring to a boil. Return
  sausage to skillet. Cover, reduce
  heat, and simmer 15 minutes.
- Serve over hot cooked pasta.

Yield: 6 servings

Low-fat turkey sausage is delicious substituted for Italian sausage.

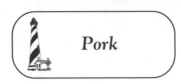

Pork

Pork Chops Pizzaiola

6 (¾-inch-thick) loin or shoulder
   pork chops, trimmed
2 tablespoons olive oil
1½ cups marinara sauce
½ teaspoon dried rosemary
½ cup sliced black olives
Salt and pepper to taste
½ cup fresh grated Parmigiano-
   Reggiano cheese

• Brown chops in hot oil in a
skillet over medium heat; drain.
Stir in marinara sauce and next
3 ingredients. Cover, reduce
heat, and simmer 30 minutes.
Uncover and simmer 15 minutes
or until meat is tender. Sprinkle
with cheese.

Yield: 6 servings

BBQ Sauce

½ cup vegetable oil
1 medium onion
¾ cup ketchup
¾ cup water
⅓ cup lemon juice
3 tablespoons Worcestershire
   sauce
2 tablespoons prepared mustard
2 teaspoons salt
½ teaspoon pepper
3 tablespoons sugar

This sauce is also wonderful with pork.

• Process all ingredients in a
blender until smooth. Simmer in
a saucepan 1 hour.

Yield: enough sauce for 1 chicken

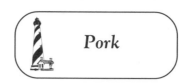

Pork Tenderloin with Mushrooms

1 (1½-pound) pork tenderloin, trimmed and cut into 2-inch-thick slices

2 tablespoons vegetable oil

1 tablespoon lemon juice

Ground pepper to taste

1 garlic clove, crushed (optional)

½ cup unsalted butter

1 onion, finely chopped

2 (8-ounce) package fresh mushrooms, thinly sliced

¼ cup dry sherry

1 cup whipping cream

Hot cooked rice

- Flatten pork slices between 2 sheets of wax paper using a meat mallet or rolling pin; arrange in a shallow baking dish.
- Combine oil, lemon juice, pepper to taste, and, if desired, garlic, stirring well. Spoon over pork, and chill 30 minutes or overnight.
- Melt butter in a skillet over medium heat; add onion, and sauté 5 minutes or until tender. Add mushrooms, and sauté until tender. Remove from skillet, reserving drippings; keep vegetables warm.
- Remove pork from marinade, discarding marinade. Cook pork in reserved drippings 1½ to 2 minutes on each side or until done; transfer to a hot serving dish, and keep warm.
- Cook sherry in skillet over medium-high heat, stirring constantly, until reduced to 2 tablespoons. Return onion and mushrooms to skillet, and season with salt and pepper to taste. Stir in cream; bring almost to a boil over medium heat, stirring constantly. Pour sauce over pork. Serve surrounded by hot cooked rice.

Yield: 6 servings

BBQ Pork

1 fresh ham (not cured or
    smoked)
Vinegar
Seasoned pepper

- Trim ham, leaving a small amount of fat. Rub with vinegar, and cover completely with seasoned pepper, pressing into sides. Wrap tightly with aluminum foil.
- Bake at 200° for 10 hours or until pork falls apart; shred meat. Serve with your favorite barbecue sauce.

This recipe is great because it cooks while you sleep or are at work.

Chicken Elegant

3 bone-in chicken breasts
Celery tops
Onion salt to taste
1 bay leaf
Dried rosemary to taste
½ cup butter or margarine
1 cup chicken broth
2 cups sour cream
1 (4-ounce) can sliced
    mushrooms
1 (10¾-ounce) cream of
    mushroom soup, undiluted
1 small package herb-seasoned
    stuffing mix

- Bring first 5 ingredients and water to cover to a boil in a large saucepan; boil 40 minutes or until chicken is done. Let cool. Bone chicken; cut meat into bite-size pieces, and place in a 9 x 13 x 2-inch baking dish.
- Cook butter and broth in a small saucepan over medium heat until butter is melted; pour over chicken. Stir in sour cream, mushrooms, and mushroom soup. Sprinkle top with stuffing mix.
- Bake at 350° for 45 minutes.

Yield: 8 servings

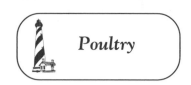

Chicken Breasts Stuffed with Spinach

3 skinned and boned chicken
  breasts, halved
Salt to taste
1 cup chopped cooked spinach,
  well drained
¾ cup ricotta cheese
¼ cup minced prosciutto
1 large egg, lightly beaten
3 tablespoons heavy cream
Salt to taste
Nutmeg to taste
¼ cup butter or margarine
⅓ cup dry white wine
⅓ cup chicken broth
Ground pepper to taste

- Flatten chicken breast halves slightly between 2 sheets of wax paper using a meat mallet or a rolling pin. Sprinkle with salt to taste.
- Combine spinach, next 5 ingredients, and salt to taste. Place ⅓ cup spinach mixture on the boned side of each breast half; fold the chicken over the filling, pressing edges together well. Cover chicken, and chill at least 1 hour.
- Preheat oven to 350°.
- Melt butter in a large ovenproof saucepan over medium heat; place chicken in pan in a single layer. Add wine and chicken broth, and bring to a boil. Bake at 350° for 15 minutes, basting with drippings 3 times. Change oven temperature to broil. Broil, turning occasionally, 5 minutes or until skin is golden. Arrange chicken on a hot serving platter.
- Cook drippings over high heat until reduced by one-fourth; season with salt and pepper to taste. Pour sauce over chicken, and serve immediately.

Yield: 6 servings

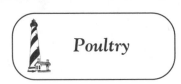

RD's Kung Pao Chicken or Shrimp

5 teaspoons soy sauce, divided

5 teaspoons dry sherry, divided

3½ teaspoons cornstarch, divided

¼ teaspoon salt

2 skinned and boned chicken breasts, cut into 2 x 3-inch strips or ½ pound medium-size fresh shrimp, peeled

1 tablespoon red wine vinegar

2 tablespoons chicken broth

1½ teaspoons sugar

⅓ cup peanuts

3 tablespoons vegetable or chile-flavored oil

1½ teaspoons minced fresh ginger

2 green onions, cut into 1-inch pieces

Hot cooked rice

- Combine 2 teaspoons soy sauce, 2 teaspoons sherry, 2 teaspoons cornstarch, and salt in a large bowl, stirring well; add chicken, stirring to coat. Let stand at room temperature 30 minutes; set aside.
- Combine remaining 3 teaspoons soy sauce, remaining 3 teaspoons sherry, remaining 1½ teaspoons cornstarch, vinegar, broth, and sugar in a small bowl, stirring well; set aside.
- Cook peanuts in 1 tablespoon hot oil in a wok or large skillet over medium heat until browned. Remove and set aside.
- Stir-fry chicken in remaining 2 tablespoons hot oil in wok 2 minutes. Add ginger, and cook 1 minute or until chicken is done. Remove from wok.
- Add green onions and reserved peanuts to wok; stir in reserved sugar mixture, and bring to a boil, stirring constantly. Boil, stirring constantly, until thickened. Add chicken mixture, stirring to coat. Serve over hot cooked rice.

Yield: 6 servings

For added heat in this recipe, stir-fry chiles in 1 tablespoon hot oil before adding chicken until charred. Add chicken, and proceed as directed.

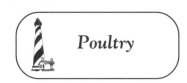
Chicken in Wine-Herb Sauce

2½ tablespoons tomato paste

2 tablespoons red wine vinegar

2 bay leaves

1 teaspoon dried rosemary

1½ cups dry red wine

2½ pounds skinned and boned
   chicken breasts

½ to ¾ cup all-purpose flour

Salt and pepper to taste

½ cup butter or margarine,
   divided

¼ cup vegetable oil

1 garlic clove, chopped

Garnish: ¼ cup chopped fresh
   parsley

- Combine first 5 ingredients in a small bowl; set aside.
- Flatten chicken breasts slightly using the heel of your hand; dry with paper towels. Dredge in flour seasoned with salt and pepper to taste. Let stand 5 minutes, and dredge again.
- Melt 3 tablespoons butter and 2 tablespoons oil in a large skillet over medium heat; add half of chicken, and cook until golden brown, turning once. Repeat procedure with 3 tablespoons butter, remaining 2 tablespoons oil, and remaining chicken. Place chicken in a shallow baking dish in a single layer, reserving drippings in skillet.
- Sauté garlic in reserved drippings in skillet until golden; add wine mixture, and bring to a gentle boil. Cook until mixture is reduced and thickened. Remove from heat, and stir in remaining 2 tablespoons butter. Pour over chicken, turning to coat. Cool. Chill up to 2 days.
- Serve cold or bake at 350° for 20 to 30 minutes. Garnish, if desired.

Yield: 6 servings

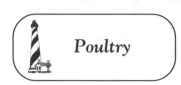
Marinated Chicken Pizza

½ cup sliced green onions, divided

2 tablespoons olive or vegetable oil, divided

2 garlic cloves, minced

2 tablespoons reduced-sodium soy sauce

2 tablespoons rice or white vinegar

½ teaspoon dried crushed red pepper

½ teaspoon ground black pepper

12 ounces skinned and boned chicken breasts, cut into ½-inch pieces

1 tablespoon cornstarch

1 (16-ounce) Italian bread shell

½ cup (2 ounces) shredded mozzarella cheese

½ cup (2 ounces) shredded Monterey Jack cheese

2 tablespoons pine nuts (optional)

- Combine ¼ cup green onions, 1 tablespoon oil, garlic, and next 4 ingredients in a large bowl; add chicken, stirring to coat. Let stand at room temperature 30 minutes. Remove chicken from marinade, reserving marinade.
- Cook chicken in remaining 1 tablespoon hot oil in a large skillet over medium heat, stirring often, 3 minutes or until no longer pink.
- Stir cornstarch into reserved marinade; add to skillet. Cook, stirring constantly, until thickened and bubbly. Spoon mixture evenly onto bread shell. Sprinkle with cheeses.
- Bake at 400° for 12 minutes. Top with remaining ¼ cup green onions and, if desired, pine nuts. Bake 2 more minutes.

Yield: 6 servings

Tacos Verde

1 small onion, chopped
1 tablespoon vegetable oil
1 (8-ounce) can tomato sauce
2 pickled jalapeño peppers, rinsed, seeded, and chopped
¼ teaspoon salt
2 cups chopped cooked chicken or pork
2 cups guacamole
Taco shells
½ cup sour cream

- Sauté onion in hot oil in a skillet until tender. Stir in tomato sauce, jalapeño, and salt. Cover, reduce heat, and simmer 5 minutes. Stir in chicken, and cook until thoroughly heated; keep warm.
- Spoon guacamole evenly into taco shells; add meat mixture, and top with sour cream.

Yield: 6 servings

Fajita Marinade

½ cup olive oil
⅓ cup lime juice
1 teaspoon sugar
½ teaspoon salt
¼ teaspoon ground cumin
¼ cup soy sauce
¼ cup red wine vinegar
⅓ cup finely chopped onion
1 teaspoon dried oregano
½ teaspoon pepper
3 garlic cloves, minced
½ teaspoon paprika

- Combine all ingredients; pour marinade over 2 pounds skirt of flank steak or chicken, and chill 24 hours. Prepare meat as desired.

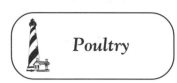
Arroz con Pollo
(or Yellow Rice and Chicken)

1 whole chicken

1 green or red bell pepper, chopped

2 medium onions, chopped

2 garlic cloves, minced

2 tablespoons vegetable oil

1 package Vigo seasoning/coloring

½ cup tomato sauce

2 bay leaves

1 pound uncooked long-grain rice

Salt to taste

1 (8-ounce) can green peas

1 (2-ounce) jar diced pimiento, drained

- Bring chicken and water to cover to a boil in a Dutch oven; boil 1 hour or until done. Drain chicken, reserving 1 quart broth. Bone chicken, and chop meat.
- Sauté bell pepper, onion, and garlic in hot oil in a skillet until tender.
- Combine chicken, reserved 1 quart broth, sautéed vegetables, seasoning package, tomato sauce, and bay leaves in Dutch oven; bring to a boil. Add rice and salt to taste; boil 5 minutes. Bake at 350° for 20 to 25 minutes.
- Heat green peas and pimiento in a small saucepan. Garnish chicken and rice with peas and pimientos.

Yield: 6 to 8 servings

Serve with salad and bread for a great meal. You may prepare chicken and broth ahead of time. You may also cook in a serving pan instead of a Dutch oven, if desired. You may substitute 1 to 1½ pounds fresh shrimp for chicken, if desired.

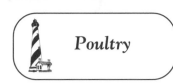

Chicken in Vinegar
with Green Peppercorns

4 skinned and boned chicken
   breasts

1 teaspoon salt

Ground black pepper

1 tablespoon plus 1½ teaspoons
   unsalted butter

1 tablespoon plus 1½ teaspoons
   vegetable oil

1 cup dry red wine

⅛ cup red wine vinegar

6 large shallots, minced

1½ garlic cloves, minced

1 bay leaf

½ teaspoon dried thyme

2 medium tomatoes, peeled,
   seeded, and coarsely chopped

1 cup beef broth

1 tablespoon plus 1½ teaspoons
   tomato paste

½ teaspoon sugar

1 tablespoon green peppercorns,
   drained

4 tablespoons unsalted butter,
   cut up

- Sprinkle chicken with salt and pepper.
- Melt 1 tablespoon plus 1½ teaspoons butter and oil in a 12-inch skillet over medium heat; add chicken, and brown, turning once. Drain chicken, and remove from skillet.
- Add wine and vinegar to skillet, and cook, stirring to loosen browned particles. Add shallots and next 3 ingredients. Simmer until reduced to ⅓ cup. Add tomato to skillet. Stir in broth, tomato paste, and sugar, mixing well. Add chicken, and simmer 10 minutes.
- Remove chicken to a hot serving platter. Pour liquid through a wire-mesh strainer, discarding solids. Boil liquid until reduced to ¾ cup. Add peppercorns; gradually add butter, stirring constantly. Season to taste, and pour sauce over chicken. Serve immediately.

Yield: 4 servings

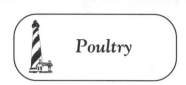
Deep-fried Chicken with Cashew Nuts

1 pound skinned and boned
   chicken breasts, cut into
   ½-inch cubes
1 egg white
2 teaspoons cornstarch, divided
1 cup cashews
6 tablespoons vegetable oil
1 teaspoon minced fresh ginger
1 teaspoon dried onion flakes
1 tablespoon cooking wine or
   sherry
1 teaspoon sugar
3 tablespoons soy sauce
1 tablespoon water
Hot cooked rice

- Combine chicken, egg white, and 1 teaspoon cornstarch in a bowl; set aside.
- Deep-fry cashews in hot oil in a wok or large skillet over medium-high heat, stirring constantly, 2 to 3 minutes or until golden. Drain.
- Sauté chicken mixture, ginger, and onion flakes in wok over medium heat until chicken is no longer pink. Combine wine, sugar, and soy sauce; stir into chicken mixture. Combine remaining 1 teaspoon cornstarch and 1 tablespoon water, stirring well; add to chicken mixture. Cook, stirring often, until thickened. Add cashews, stirring well. Serve hot with hot cooked rice.

Yield: 4 servings

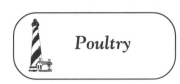
Apricot BBQ Chicken

1 (2½- to 3-pound) whole
  chicken, skinned and cut into
  pieces
½ cup apricot jam
2 tablespoons soy sauce
2 tablespoons dry white wine
2 tablespoons minced green
  onions
2 tablespoons minced garlic
2 tablespoons minced fresh
  ginger
2 tablespoons lemon juice
Salt and pepper to taste

- Combine all ingredients in a
  heavy-duty zip-top plastic bag;
  seal and turn to coat. Chill
  4 hours, turning occasionally.
  Remove chicken from marinade,
  reserving marinade.
- Grill chicken over medium heat
  (300° to 350°) 15 minutes on
  each side, basting with reserved
  marinade.

Yield: 4 to 6 servings

Aunt Joyce's Chicken in Wine Gravy

½ cup butter or margarine
2 whole chickens, cut up
½ cup chopped onion
1 pinch of thyme
1 tablespoon dried parsley flakes
3 (10¾-ounce) cans cream of
  chicken or mushroom soup,
  undiluted
1½ soup cans dry white wine
1 (4-ounce) can sliced
  mushrooms

- Melt butter in a large skillet over
  medium heat; add chicken, and
  cook until browned. Remove
  chicken from skillet, reserving
  drippings. Add onion and next
  5 ingredients to drippings;
  simmer until thoroughly heated.
- Arrange chicken in a 9 x 13 x
  2-inch baking dish; pour sauce
  over top.
- Bake at 350° for 1 hour.

Yield: 8 servings

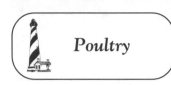
Chicken Florentine

½ (17¼-ounce) package frozen
  puff pastry sheets

2 tablespoons butter or margarine

2 skinned and boned chicken
  breasts, halved

1 (10-ounce) package frozen
  creamed spinach, thawed

¼ cup grated Parmesan cheese

¼ cup chopped toasted pine nuts

1 tablespoon chopped fresh basil

1 garlic clove, minced

1 large egg

1 tablespoon water

Grated Parmesan cheese

- Let pastry sheet stand at room temperature 20 minutes.
- Melt butter in a skillet over medium heat; add chicken, and cook until browned, turning once. Remove chicken from skillet.
- Combine spinach and next 4 ingredients in a bowl.
- Preheat oven to 375°.
- Roll pastry sheet into a 14-inch square on a lightly floured surface; cut into 4 (7-inch) squares. Spoon spinach mixture evenly into the center of each square; top each with a chicken breast half. Wrap pastry over chicken, pressing seams to seal. Place seam side down on an ungreased baking sheet.
- Whisk together egg and 1 tablespoon water; lightly brush over pastry, and sprinkle with additional Parmesan cheese.
- Bake at 375° for 20 minutes or until golden.

Yield: 4 servings

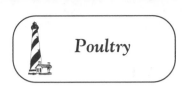
Creamy Tarragon Chicken

3 tablespoons butter or
  margarine
6 skinned and boned chicken
  breasts
1 large onion, chopped
2 (8-ounce) packages fresh
  mushrooms, sliced
1 pint whipping cream
Sliced Monterey Jack cheese
Salt and pepper to taste
1 to 2 tablespoons dried tarragon
Hot cooked rice

- Melt butter in a saucepan over medium heat; add chicken, and cook until browned, turning once. Remove from pan, reserving drippings.
- Add onion and mushrooms to pan, and sauté until tender. Add whipping cream, and cook until thickened.
- Place chicken in a single layer in a 9 x 13 x 2-inch baking dish. Top with cheese, and pour sauce over cheese. Season with salt and pepper to taste, and sprinkle with tarragon.
- Bake at 350° for 30 minutes. Serve with hot cooked rice.

Yield: 8 servings

For a variation you can flatten the chicken breasts using a meat mallet or rolling pin, and fill with chopped cooked spinach.

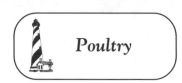

Chicken Cacciatore

2 tablespoons butter or margarine

2 tablespoons olive oil

3 skinned and boned chicken breasts, cut into bite-size pieces

2 green bell peppers, diced

1 (8-ounce) package fresh mushrooms, sliced

1 medium onion, chopped

2 garlic cloves, pressed

⅔ cup red wine

⅔ cup chicken broth

1 (6-ounce) can tomato paste

1 teaspoon salt

2 tablespoons white vinegar

¼ teaspoon dried oregano

¼ teaspoon pepper

2 bay leaves

Hot cooked bow-tie pasta

• Melt butter and oil in a large saucepan over medium-high heat; add chicken, and cook until browned, stirring often. Remove chicken from pan, reserving drippings.

• Add bell pepper and next 3 ingredients to reserved drippings; reduce heat to medium, and cook, stirring often, until tender. Add wine and next 7 ingredients, stirring well. Bring to a boil; cover, reduce heat, and simmer, stirring occasionally, 35 minutes. Return chicken to pan; cover and simmer 20 minutes or until chicken is tender. Serve over hot cooked bow-tie pasta.

Yield: 8 servings

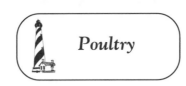

Sesame Chicken and Celery

1 bone-in chicken breast, halved
1 tablespoon dry sherry
1 tablespoon soy sauce
2 tablespoons grated fresh ginger
¼ cup chicken broth
1 teaspoon cornstarch
3 celery ribs, diagonally sliced
4 green onions, diagonally sliced
2 tablespoons vegetable oil
Hot cooked rice
2 tablespoons sesame seeds, toasted

• Skin chicken breast halves, and bone. Cut meat into 1-inch pieces.
• Combine chicken, sherry, soy sauce, and ginger in a bowl, stirring to coat. Let stand at room temperature 20 minutes.
• Combine broth and cornstarch in a separate bowl, stirring until smooth; set aside.
• Stir-fry celery and green onions in hot oil in a wok or large skillet over high heat 2 minutes or until crisp-tender; remove from wok; set aside.
• Remove chicken from marinade, reserving marinade. Stir-fry chicken in wok, adding oil as needed, 3 minutes or until browned. Combine reserved marinade and broth mixture; add to chicken, stirring well. Cook, stirring often, until thickened and bubbly. Cook, stirring constantly, 2 minutes. Stir in vegetables. Cover and cook 1 minute.
• Spoon chicken mixture over hot cooked rice, and sprinkle with sesame seeds.

Yield: 2 to 3 servings

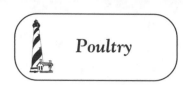

Honey-Rosemary Chicken

2 tablespoons chopped fresh
 rosemary

⅓ cup honey

2¼ tablespoons coarse-grained
 mustard

3 garlic cloves, finely chopped

¼ cup olive oil

2 teaspoons lemon juice

¼ teaspoon freshly ground
 pepper

Salt to taste

4 bone-in chicken breasts, halved

- Stir together first 8 ingredients.
 Place chicken in a single layer in
 a shallow baking dish; pour
 marinade over top. Chill several
 hours. Remove chicken from
 marinade, reserving marinade.
- Grill chicken over low heat
 (250° to 300°) 40 to 45 minutes,
 basting with reserved marinade.

Yield: 8 servings

Grandma's Turkey Stuffing

1 large onion, chopped

1 celery rib with leaves, chopped

¾ cup butter or margarine,
 melted

½ teaspoon salt

Dash of freshly ground pepper

1 tablespoon chopped fresh
 parsley

2 cups diced apple

¼ cup raisins

1 cup chopped nuts

5 cups cubed stale bread
 moistened with a little water

- Combine all ingredients, stirring
 well.
- Stuff lightly in chicken or
 turkey. Bake chicken or turkey
 according to package directions.

*Yield: enough stuffing for a
10-pound turkey or chicken*

This stuffing can be used with chicken or turkey.

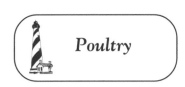
Oyster Dressing

1 cup butter or margarine,
  divided

1 cup chopped celery

1½ cups chopped onion

4 cups crumbled dry bread or
  biscuits

1 quart oysters, undrained

½ cup milk

1 teaspoon sage

2 teaspoons salt

⅛ teaspoon pepper

- Melt ½ cup butter in a skillet over medium heat; add celery and onion, and sauté until tender. Combine onion mixture and biscuit crumbs in a large bowl.
- Melt remaining ½ cup butter in skillet over medium heat; add oysters, and cook until edges begin to curl. Remove oysters from skillet, and pour liquid over crumb mixture. Chop oysters, and add to crumb mixture. Stir in milk and next 3 ingredients, adding more milk as needed.
- Stuff lightly in turkey. Bake turkey according to package directions.

*Yield: enough dressing for
a 10-pound turkey*

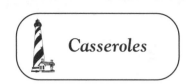

Wild Rice-Chicken Casserole

1 package wild rice mix

1 tablespoon butter or margarine

½ cup chopped onion

½ cup sliced fresh mushrooms

1 envelope Hollandaise sauce mix

⅔ cup water

2 cups chopped cooked chicken

1 package frozen chopped
   broccoli, cooked

- Prepare rice according to package directions.
- Melt butter in a skillet over medium heat; add onion and mushrooms, and sauté until tender. Add sauce mix and ⅔ cup water; cook, stirring constantly, until thickened.
- Combine rice, chicken, and broccoli in a greased 7 x 11 x 2-inch baking dish; spoon sauce mixture over top.
- Bake, covered, at 350° for 35 minutes.

Yield: 4 to 6 servings

Sausage Casserole

1 (16-ounce) package sausage

2 cups chopped celery

1 cup chopped onion

1 cup cooked rice

1 (10¾-ounce) can cream of
   chicken soup, undiluted

1 (10¾-ounce) can cream of
   celery soup, undiluted

¼ cup chopped green bell pepper

1 small can mushrooms

- Brown sausage in a skillet over medium heat, stirring until it crumbles and is no longer pink; drain. Add celery and onion, and cook 3 minutes. Stir in rice and next 4 ingredients; simmer 2 minutes. Spoon mixture into a 7 x 11 x 2-inch baking dish.
- Bake at 350° for 35 minutes.

Yield: 6 servings

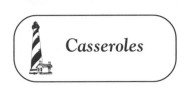
Beef Stroganoff

¼ cup butter or margarine

¼ cup chopped onion

1 garlic clove, chopped

1 (8-ounce) package fresh
mushrooms

1 pound lean round steak, cut
into bite-size pieces

1 can beef consommé, undiluted

1 teaspoon salt

¼ teaspoon pepper

3 tablespoons lemon juice

4 ounces fine egg noodles,
uncooked

1 cup sour cream

This casserole is great for company.

• Melt butter in a skillet over
medium heat; add onion, garlic,
and mushrooms, and sauté until
tender. Add steak, and cook
until done. Stir in consommé
and next 3 ingredients; reduce
heat, and simmer 15 minutes.
Stir in noodles, and cook 20
minutes or until noodles are
tender. Stir in sour cream, and
serve immediately.

Yield: 6 servings

Tamale Pie

1 medium onion, chopped

1 garlic clove, minced

1 pound lean ground beef or turkey

1 tablespoon olive oil

1½ teaspoons chili powder

Salt and pepper to taste

1 (16-ounce) can corn

1 (16-ounce) can red kidney beans

1 (16-ounce) can tomatoes, chopped

1 (16-ounce) can pitted ripe olives, drained

1 (10-ounce) mild enchilada sauce

1 (16-ounce) can tamales, peeled and cut into 1-inch pieces or 3 cups nacho cheese chips

1 cup (4 ounces) shredded Cheddar cheese

• Cook first 3 ingredients in hot oil in a skillet over medium heat, stirring until meat crumbles and is no longer pink. Stir in chili powder and salt and pepper to taste; spoon mixture into a 9 x 13 x 2-inch baking dish. Stir in corn and next 5 ingredients just until blended. Sprinkle with cheese.

• Bake at 350° for 40 to 45 minutes or until the middle is bubbly.

Yield: 8 servings

This is an easy dish to take to new neighbors, to prepare for unexpected company, or to have ready after a day at the beach.

Chicken-Squash Casserole

1 (2½- to 3-pound) whole
chicken

2 pounds yellow squash, cut into
¼-inch-thick slices

½ cup water

2 large carrots, shredded

1 red bell pepper, chopped

1 medium onion, finely chopped

1 (8-ounce) container sour
cream

1 (10¾-ounce) can cream of
mushroom soup, undiluted

½ teaspoon salt

¼ teaspoon pepper

1½ cups chicken-flavored one-
step stuffing mix

¼ cup butter or margarine,
melted

- Cook chicken in boiling water to cover in a Dutch oven 45 minutes or until tender; drain. Let cool. Skin and bone; cut meat into bite-size pieces.
- Bring squash and ½ cup water to a boil in a saucepan; cover, reduce heat, and simmer 8 minutes or until tender. Drain, pressing between layers of paper towels. Combine squash, carrot, bell pepper, and onion, tossing gently.
- Combine sour cream and next 3 ingredients in a large bowl; add chicken and squash mixture, stirring to blend. Spoon mixture into a lightly greased 9 x 13 x 2-inch baking dish.
- Combine stuffing mix and butter; sprinkle over casserole.
- Bake at 350° for 25 minutes or until bubbly.

Yield: 8 servings

For chicken-flavored one-step stuffing mix, we used Stove Top One-Step Stuffing Mix.

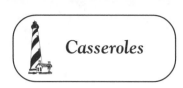
Cabbage Rolls

1 large cabbage, cored
1 pound ground beef
½ pound ground pork or pork
   sausage
½ teaspoon salt
½ teaspoon pepper
1 large egg, lightly beaten
½ cup uncooked rice
1 can tomato soup, undiluted
1 large can sauerkraut

- Arrange cabbage in a steamer basket over boiling water; cover and steam until leaves are pliable. Remove from heat, and carefully peel off leaves. Combine beef and next 6 ingredients, mixing well by hand. Place a heaping tablespoon of beef mixture on each cabbage leaf; roll up, and fold securely.
- Place 1 layer of sauerkraut in a 4- to 5-quart Dutch oven; place cabbage rolls on sauerkraut, and layer until all is used. Cover with water; simmer, covered, 1 hour or until meat is done.

Yield: 6 to 10 cabbage rolls

If desired, bake cabbage rolls, covered, at 350° for 1 hour.

Seafood

St. Augustine Lighthouse

The Ancient City's first skyscraper and oldest surviving brick building was begun in 1872, finished in 1874, and soon joined by a duplex brick lightkeepers' house. This complex replaced an earlier coquina tower which was undermined by erosion and finally toppled into the ocean in 1880.

Originally powered by lard oil, and later by kerosene, the light was not electrified until 1936. The lighthouse was automated in 1955 when the last full-time keeper retired.

The empty lightkeepers' house was gutted by fire in 1970, left abandoned, and threatened with demolition for a decade—until the Junior Service League committed itself to the massive task of saving it. The house was turned into a museum in the 1980s, and in the 1990s the lighthouse itself was made accessible to the public.

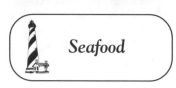

Seafood

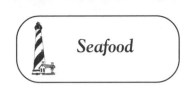

Herb Grilled Salmon

½ cup dry vermouth
½ cup vegetable oil
2 tablespoons lemon juice
¾ teaspoon salt
¼ teaspoon pepper
½ teaspoon dried thyme
½ teaspoon dried marjoram
¼ teaspoon dried sage
1 tablespoon minced fresh
   parsley
4 salmon steaks

- Combine first 9 ingredients. Place salmon in a shallow baking dish; pour marinade over top. Cover and chill 2 to 3 hours. Drain salmon, reserving marinade.
- Grill salmon over medium heat (300° to 350°) 7 to 8 minutes on each side or until fish is firm and opaque, basting with reserved marinade.

Yield: 4 servings

Old City BBQ Shrimp

6¼ pounds unpeeled, medium-
   size fresh shrimp
½ cup butter or margarine,
   melted
¼ cup Worcestershire sauce
¼ cup lemon juice
1 tablespoon Old Bay seasoning
1 tablespoon coarsely ground
   pepper
1 to 2 garlic cloves, minced
1 tablespoon Cajun seasoning
1 tablespoon hot sauce

- Peel shrimp and devein, if desired. Combine shrimp and remaining ingredients in a lightly greased large shallow roasting pan; tossing to coat. Arrange shrimp in a single layer.
- Bake at 350°, stirring occasionally, 15 to 20 minutes or until shrimp turn pink.

Yield: 25 servings

Race Point Scallops

½ cup butter or margarine
1 pound scallops or other seafood
¼ cup St. Augustine sweet onion
Cream
3 tablespoons process cheese
   spread
1 tablespoon dry sherry
1½ teaspoons cornstarch
1 tablespoon cold water
Ground nutmeg
Croutons

• Melt butter in a skillet over medium heat; add scallops and onion, and sauté until scallops are done. Add enough cream to cover scallops. Stir in cheese spread and sherry. Reduce heat, and simmer 7 to 10 minutes. Combine cornstarch and 1 tablespoon cold water, stirring until smooth; add to scallop mixture. Cook, stirring often, until thickened. Spoon mixture into individual baking dishes; sprinkle with a dash of nutmeg and crumbled croutons.
• Bake at 350° for 15 minutes.

Yield: 6 servings

Red Clam Sauce

2 cups chopped onion
12 ounces fresh mushrooms,
   sliced
6 garlic cloves, crushed
2 tablespoons olive oil
½ teaspoon salt
¼ teaspoon ground black pepper
1 (10½-ounce) can tomato puree
4 (6.5-ounce) cans clams, minced
   and drained with liquid
   reserved
⅛ teaspoon ground red pepper

• Sauté first 3 ingredients in hot oil in a large saucepan until tender. Stir in salt and next 4 ingredients. Cover and cook, stirring occasionally, 45 minutes. Serve over cooked pasta.

Yield: 8 cups

This recipe is both low-fat and low-cal.

Oyster Spaghetti

2 bunches shallots or green
   onions, chopped

1 large onion, chopped

1 large green bell pepper,
   chopped

2 garlic cloves, minced

1 bunch fresh parsley, chopped

3 celery ribs, chopped

Vegetable oil

¼ teaspoon ground thyme

3 bay leaves

2 (8-ounce) cans tomato sauce

2 teaspoons salt

½ teaspoon pepper

2 (4-ounce) cans button or sliced
   mushrooms or 1 (8-ounce)
   package fresh mushrooms,
   sliced and sautéed in butter

4 dozen raw oysters or
   4 (12-ounce) jars oysters,
   drained with liquid reserved
   (cut in half if large)

12 ounces vermicelli, cooked

2½ cups (10 ounces) shredded
   sharp Cheddar cheese

Freshly grated Parmesan cheese

- Sauté first 6 ingredients in hot oil in a skillet until tender; add thyme and next 4 ingredients. Reduce heat, and simmer, partially covered, 30 minutes. Stir in mushrooms, oysters, and reserved liquid; cook 15 minutes. Adjust seasonings to taste.
- Combine oyster sauce, hot cooked pasta, and 2 cups Cheddar cheese in a large bowl, mixing thoroughly. Spoon mixture into a 9 x 13 x 2-inch baking dish. Sprinkle with remaining ½ cup Cheddar cheese.
- Bake, covered, at 350° for 30 minutes. Let stand at room temperature 10 minutes. Sprinkle each serving with Parmesan cheese.

Yield: 16 servings

Snapper Veronique

2 snapper fillets
¾ cup clam juice
¾ cup dry white wine
1 shallot, chopped
¼ cup heavy cream
Salt and ground black pepper
   to taste
Ground red pepper
2 egg yolks
1 tablespoon heavy cream
½ cup sliced mushrooms
½ cup sliced white grapes

- Bring water to a boil in a large skillet over medium heat. Reduce heat, and add fillets; cover and simmer until tender. Drain, reserving liquid.
- Cook clam juice and next 5 ingredients in a saucepan over medium heat until reduced by half.
- Whisk egg yolks in the top of a double boiler; bring water to a boil. Cook, whisking constantly, until ribbons form. Stir in 1 tablespoon cream. Stir in reserved poaching liquid. Add mushrooms, and cook until thoroughly heated (do not boil).
- Place snapper in a roasting pan; pour sauce over top. Top with grapes. Broil until lightly browned. Serve immediately.

Yield: 2 servings

Crab Cakes

1 pound backfin crabmeat
2 large eggs, lightly beaten
¼ cup finely chopped onion
½ cup cracker crumbs
3 tablespoons mayonnaise
1 tablespoon prepared mustard
Butter

- Combine first 6 ingredients. Shape mixture into patties.
- Melt butter in a skillet over medium heat; add patties, and sauté until golden brown.

Yield: 4 to 6 servings

Shrimp Elegante

12 pounds unpeeled, large fresh shrimp

2 cups butter or margarine

3 cups olive oil

12 onions, coarsely chopped

12 garlic cloves, crushed

1½ bunches fresh parsley, chopped

4 teaspoons dried oregano

2 cups dry white wine

1⅓ cups Italian dressing

1 cup water

5 tablespoons plus 1 teaspoon chicken bouillon granules

Freshly ground pepper to taste

48 ounces linguine, uncooked

3 tablespoons vegetable oil

Garnishes: fresh parsley sprigs, lemon slices

- Peel shrimp and devein, if desired; butterfly shrimp. Cook shrimp in boiling salted water to cover in a large Dutch oven 30 seconds. Drain and place in a shallow broiling pan.
- Melt butter and oil in a skillet over medium heat; add onion and next 3 ingredients. Cook, stirring occasionally, until tender. Add wine and next 4 ingredients, stirring until bouillon is dissolved. Reduce heat to low, and cook 5 minutes. Pour mixture over shrimp. Cover and chill.
- Cook linguine according to package directions; add 3 tablespoons oil to the cooking water. Drain but do not rinse.
- Uncover shrimp, and broil 4 inches from heat, 5 minutes on each side or until done. Arrange hot cooked pasta on serving plates. Serve shrimp over pasta, spooning no more than 2 tablespoons juice over top of each serving. Garnish, if desired. Serve immediately.

Yield: 24 servings

The shrimp can be peeled, deveined, and butterflied the night before; however, be sure to refrigerate them in either a glass or plastic container.

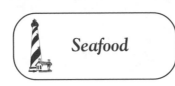

Stuffed Flounder Fillets

2 tablespoons butter or margarine

⅔ cup finely chopped celery

1 medium onion, finely chopped

1 pound medium-size fresh
  shrimp, cooked, peeled, and
  chopped

½ cup fresh lump crabmeat,
  drained

½ cup seasoned breadcrumbs

1 tablespoon chopped fresh
  parsley

1 large egg, lightly beaten

6 flounder or sole fillets

White Wine Sauce

Breadcrumbs, buttered

Grated Parmesan cheese

Chopped fresh parsley

• Melt butter in a skillet over
  medium heat; add celery and
  onion, and sauté until tender.
  Stir in shrimp and next 4
  ingredients.
• Spread shrimp mixture evenly
  over fillets; roll up, and place in
  a lightly greased baking dish.
  Pour White Wine Sauce over
  fillets. Top with breadcrumbs,
  Parmesan cheese, and chopped
  fresh parsley. Chill overnight, if
  desired.
• Bake at 350° for 30 minutes.

White Wine Sauce

2 tablespoons butter or margarine

2 tablespoons all-purpose flour

2 cups milk

¼ teaspoon salt

Ground white pepper

1 (2-ounce) can sliced
  mushrooms, drained

¼ cup dry white wine

• Melt butter in a saucepan over
  medium heat; add flour, stirring
  until smooth. Add milk; cook,
  stirring constantly, until
  thickened. Remove from heat;
  stir in salt and next 3
  ingredients.

Yield: 2½ cups
Yield: 6 servings

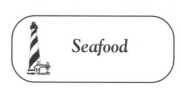

Shrimp Creole

12 ounces unpeeled, medium-size fresh shrimp

½ cup chopped onion

½ cup chopped celery

1 garlic clove, minced

3 tablespoons vegetable oil

1 (16-ounce) can tomatoes

1 (8-ounce) can tomato sauce

1½ teaspoons salt

1 teaspoon sugar

½ to 1 teaspoon chili powder

1 tablespoon Worcestershire sauce

Dash of hot sauce

2 teaspoons cornstarch

1 tablespoon cold water

½ cup chopped green bell pepper

Hot cooked rice

- Peel shrimp and devein, if desired.
- Cook onion, celery, and garlic in hot oil in a skillet over medium heat until tender. Stir in tomatoes and next 6 ingredients; simmer uncovered 45 minutes.
- Combine cornstarch and 1 tablespoon water, stirring until smooth; stir into tomato sauce. Cook, stirring constantly, until thickened and bubbly. Stir in shrimp and bell pepper. Cover, reduce heat, and simmer 5 minutes. Serve over hot cooked rice.

Yield: 8 servings

Shrimp Pilau

2 pounds unpeeled, medium-size
  fresh shrimp
½ pound white bacon
2 medium onions, chopped
1 green bell pepper
1 datil pepper, chopped
  (if unavailable, use hot sauce
  to taste)
1 large can tomatoes
2 bay leaves
8 to 10 whole cloves
½ teaspoon ground thyme
Salt and pepper to taste
3 cups water
3 cups uncooked rice

• Peel shrimp, and devein, if desired.
• Cook bacon in a Dutch oven over low heat until fat separates and bacon is crisp; add onion and peppers, and sauté until lightly browned. Add tomatoes and next 4 ingredients. Cook until thickened.
• Add shrimp and 3 cups water to tomato mixture and bring to a boil; boil 5 minutes. Add rice and bring to a boil. Reduce heat and simmer, stirring often, 15 to 20 minutes or until liquid is absorbed. Remove from heat and let stand 30 minutes. Transfer mixture to a serving dish.

Yield: 6 to 8 servings

Shrimp Casserole

6 bread slices, torn into pieces
1½ pounds cooked shrimp,
  peeled
2 cups (8 ounces) shredded sharp
  Cheddar cheese
¼ cup butter or margarine,
  melted
½ teaspoon dry mustard
3 large eggs, lightly beaten
2 cups milk

• Combine first 3 ingredients in a 2-quart baking dish; pour melted butter over top. Stir in dry mustard, eggs, and milk. Chill overnight.
• Bake, covered, at 350° for 1 hour.

Yield: 6 servings

Fish and Chip Bake

4 to 5 medium potatoes, boiled
  and mashed
1 (10-ounce) package chopped
  spinach, cooked and well
  drained
½ cup sour cream
Dash of pepper
1 pound perch, flounder, or other
  mild fish fillets
¼ cup milk
½ cup herb-seasoned stuffing
  mix, crushed
2 tablespoons butter or
  margarine, melted
Lemon slices

• Combine first 4 ingredients;
  spoon into a 6 x 10 x 2-inch
  baking dish.
• Dip 1 side of each fillet in milk
  and dredge in stuffing mix. Fold
  fillets in half, stuffing side out.
  Place on top of potato mixture
  and drizzle with melted butter.
• Bake uncovered at 350° for 30 to
  45 minutes or until fish flakes
  easily with a fork. Serve with
  lemon slices.

Yield: 4 to 5 servings

Shrimp Fra Diavolo

2 pounds unpeeled, medium-size
  fresh shrimp
2 tablespoons butter or margarine
½ teaspoon garlic salt
30 ounces marinara sauce
⅛ teaspoon ground red pepper
3 to 4 drops hot sauce
1 small can mushrooms pieces
Salt to taste
16 ounces fusilli pasta, cooked

• Peel shrimp, and devein, if
  desired.
• Melt butter in a large skillet over
  medium heat; add shrimp and
  sauté 3 minutes. Stir in garlic
  salt. Remove shrimp from skillet.
• Simmer marinara sauce and next
  4 ingredients in skillet 5
  minutes; add shrimp and cook,
  stirring often, 2 minutes. Serve
  sauce over hot cooked pasta.

Yield: 6 to 8 servings

Lobster Thermidor

1 cup fish stock

½ cup dry white wine

1 onion, peeled and quartered

4 peppercorns

1 bay leaf

1 thyme sprig

Salt and pepper to taste

1½ cups milk

3 (1¼- to 1½-pound) lobsters, cooked

½ cup unsalted butter, divided

¼ cup all-purpose flour

1 teaspoon Dijon mustard

2 egg yolks

½ cup half-and-half

1 teaspoon lemon juice

3 ounces grated Parmesan cheese

¼ cup toasted breadcrumbs

- Bring stock and wine to a boil in a saucepan; boil until reduced to ½ cup.
- Bring onion and next 5 ingredients to a boil in a separate saucepan. Remove from heat and cover. Let stand at room temperature 30 minutes.
- Remove claws from lobsters; split each body in half lengthwise. Set shells aside with the feeler claws intact. Discard the gray sack in the head and the black intestinal tube in the body. Run any loose coral (or spawn) through a wire-mesh strainer. Remove the meat from the shells and the claws. Cut meat carefully into ¾-inch cubes.
- Melt ¼ cup butter in a heavy skillet over medium heat; add lobster meat and cook, turning often, 3 to 4 minutes. Remove lobster meat from skillet.
- Melt remaining ¼ cup butter in skillet over medium heat; stir in flour and cook over low heat 2 minutes. Remove from heat.
- Pour milk mixture through a wire-mesh strainer, discarding solids. Gradually add milk and stock mixtures to roux, stirring until smooth. Bring to a boil, stirring constantly. Cook

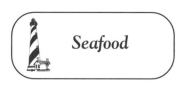
(Lobster Thermidor continued)

3 minutes or until thickened. Remove from heat and let stand 2 minutes. Stir in strained coral, mustard, yolks, and half-and-half. Season with salt and pepper to taste. Stir in lemon juice.
- Coat the inside of the empty lobster shells with a small amount of sauce. Combine half the remaining sauce and lobster meat; spoon evenly into shells. Cover evenly with remaining sauce. Combine Parmesan cheese and breadcrumbs; sprinkle over lobsters.
- Broil until topping is golden brown. Serve lobster on a bed of lettuce. Crisp French bread and a tossed green salad are traditional accompaniments.

Yield: 6 servings

Lobster is the most expensive of all shellfish, but is also regarded by gourmets as the most delicious. This classic French recipe comes from the famous Cafe de Paris.

Scallops in a Shell

½ cup butter

2 pounds scallops, shrimp, or lobster, drained

1 green onion, finely chopped

1 cup heavy whipping cream

2 tablespoons all-purpose flour

3 tablespoons shredded Cheddar cheese

2 tablespoons pale dry sherry

Salt and pepper to taste

½ cup cheese croutons, finely crushed

Dried parsley flakes

- Melt butter in a saucepan over medium heat; add scallops and sauté 3 to 4 minutes. Add green onion and sauté until tender.
- Combine cream and flour in a jar; cover tightly and shake vigorously. Pour cream mixture into scallop mixture and cook, stirring constantly, until thickened. Add cheese and sherry, stirring until smooth and creamy. Simmer 10 minutes. Season with salt and pepper to taste.
- Spoon scallop mixture into small scallop shells or individual baking dishes coated with vegetable cooking spray. Top with crushed croutons and parsley flakes.
- Bake on a baking sheet at 325° for 15 to 20 minutes.

Yield: 6 to 8 servings

This is a very easy dish to make, and cooking it in real scallop shells makes a very impressive dinner party.

St. Augustine's Secret – The Datil Pepper

The Datil Pepper

The Datil Pepper is as unique to St. John's County as any other feature of our special area. It is a very hot, small green pepper that is used in many local recipes and is only grown in St. John's County. The plant will grow in other areas but not with the same heat intensity or distinct flavor as it has when it is produced here. There are several myths as to how the pepper came to our area. Whether it came with the Spanish settlers or with the Minorcans, we're glad that it got here. This pepper must be used sparingly due to its incredible heat. Although any hot pepper can be substituted in the following recipes, a true Datil pepper fan would not approve. Once you've tasted this delectable pepper, that's it. You're hooked! Only Datil Peppers will do.

Use caution when handling Datil peppers. It is recommended that rubber gloves be worn while chopping them as the juice can burn your skin. They can be stored by drying them or freezing them. We would suggest that the seeds be removed before freezing them as they are difficult to remove after the pepper is thawed and soft. There are several Datil pepper products available in many grocery and specialty stores.

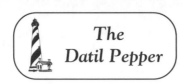

The Datil Pepper

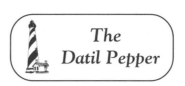
Minorcan Clam Chowder

2 pounds onions, finely chopped
Vegetable oil
2 (28-ounce) cans tomatoes,
   drained
½ datil pepper, minced
1 garlic clove, minced
2 pounds white potatoes, cubed
Dried thyme to taste
Salt and pepper to taste
1 quart fresh minced clams,
   ground

• Cook onion in hot oil in a skillet over medium heat until browned. Add tomatoes, datil pepper, and garlic; reduce heat, and cook until a paste.
• Boil potato in water to cover in a Dutch oven 20 minutes or until tender; stir potato and cooking water into tomato mixture. Stir in thyme, salt, and pepper to taste.
• Cook ground clams in water to cover in a medium saucepan over medium heat 20 minutes; add clams and cooking water to tomato mixture, stirring well. Cook until thoroughly heated. Serve hot.

Yield: about 3 quarts

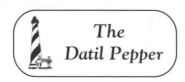
Spanish Bean Soup

2 pounds garbanzo beans

2 large onions, minced

½ cup olive oil

1 large bell pepper, finely
    chopped

1 (14-ounce) can tomatoes,
    finely chopped

1 garlic clove, halved

2 datil peppers

2 pounds Spanish sausage, cut
    into 2-inch pieces

- Soak beans overnight in water to
  cover; drain.
- Sauté onion in hot oil in a
  skillet until tender.
- Bring beans and water to a depth
  2 inches above beans to a boil in
  a Dutch oven; boil until tender.
  Reduce heat, and simmer. Add
  bell pepper and tomatoes,
  stirring well. Stir in onion,
  garlic, and datil peppers. Stir in
  sausage, and cook over medium-
  low heat until sausage is
  completely cooked, adding water
  as needed. (Soup should be
  thick.) Remove and discard
  peppers. Serve hot.

Datil Crab Cakes

1 pound fresh lump crabmeat,
    drained

2 large eggs

½ celery rib, finely chopped

2 large onions, finely chopped

Dash of datil pepper sauce

1 pinch of ground black pepper

10 saltine crackers, crushed

2 tablespoons butter or
    margarine, melted

- Combine first 7 ingredients,
  stirring to blend. Form into
  patties, and place on a rack in a
  roasting pan. Brush with melted
  butter, and broil 4 minutes on
  each side or until golden brown
  (watch carefully so as not to
  burn).

Yield: 4 to 6 servings

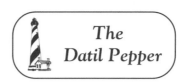
Shrimp Tolliver

1 pound unpeeled, small fresh
  shrimp
¼ cup olive oil
3 tablespoons lemon juice
2 cups uncooked rice
2 tablespoons chopped fresh
  chives
¼ teaspoon saffron
2 tablespoons butter or margarine
1 garlic clove
½ cup chopped almonds
Dash of datil pepper sauce
2 tablespoons dry vermouth

- Peel shrimp, and devein.
  Combine oil and lemon juice in
  a shallow dish; add shrimp,
  tossing to coat. Chill 2 hours,
  turning once.
- Prepare rice with chives and
  saffron according to rice package
  directions.
- Drain shrimp, reserving
  marinade. Melt butter in a
  skillet over medium heat; add
  shrimp and garlic, and cook
  until shrimp turn pink. Remove
  and discard garlic; transfer
  shrimp to a hot serving platter,
  reserving drippings. Add
  almonds, reserved marinade,
  pepper sauce, and vermouth to
  drippings; cook until thoroughly
  heated (do not boil). Pour over
  shrimp.
- Serve shrimp and sauce over
  rice.

Yield: 3 servings

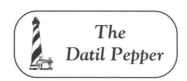

Minorcan Shrimp Pilau

2 pounds unpeeled, medium-size
 fresh shrimp

⅓ pound bacon

4 medium onions, chopped

1 (16-ounce) can sliced or
 chopped tomatoes, drained

1 small green or red bell pepper,
 chopped

1 datil pepper, finely chopped

3 cups water

2 cups uncooked rice

- Peel shrimp, and devein.
- Cook bacon and onion in a large
  Dutch oven over medium-low
  heat until bacon is crispy.
  Transfer half of bacon to a plate,
  and set aside.
- Add tomatoes to onion mixture,
  and cook 3 minutes. Add bell
  pepper and datil pepper, and
  cook until vegetables are
  browned. Add shrimp, and cook
  2 to 3 minutes. Add 3 cups
  water, and bring to a boil over
  medium-high heat. Add rice;
  cover, reduce heat, and simmer
  20 minutes or until rice is tender
  and fluffy (follow time on rice
  package). Crumble reserved half
  of bacon, and sprinkle over each
  serving.

Yield: 4 to 6 servings

Datil Pepper Vinegar

Whole datil peppers
Vinegar

- Fill a jar or bottle with datil
  peppers; cover with vinegar. Let
  stand 1 to 2 days. To serve
  sprinkle over vegetables, fish,
  rice dishes, etc. The datil flavor
  will sustain 2 to 3 vinegar refills.

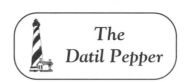

Shrimp Puppies

1 pound unpeeled, medium-size
    fresh shrimp
1 red or green bell pepper
3 small celery ribs
1 medium onion
3 fresh parsley sprigs
3 tablespoons all-purpose flour
2 large eggs, lightly beaten
1 teaspoon salt
Ground red pepper to taste
Ground black pepper to taste
Shortening
Datil pepper sauce

- Peel shrimp, and devein.
- Process shrimp and next 4 ingredients in a food processor until chopped.
- Combine flour and enough water to make a thin paste in a bowl; add eggs, stirring well. Add shrimp mixture, salt, and ground red and black pepper to taste, stirring until blended.
- Heat shortening to 375° in a large Dutch oven; drop batter by spoonfuls into hot oil, and fry until golden brown. Drain on paper towels. Serve puppies hot with datil pepper sauce.

Yield: about 20 "puppies"

Chicken Pilau

¼ cup shortening
1 pound onions, finely chopped
1 (28-ounce) can tomatoes
½ teaspoon sugar
1 teaspoon salt
1 pinch of ground black pepper
1 datil pepper
1 teaspoon chopped fresh thyme
1 whole chicken, cut into pieces
1 pound uncooked rice, rinsed
2 cups water

- Melt shortening in a large Dutch oven over medium heat; add onion, and cook until browned. Stir in tomatoes and next 5 ingredients, and cook until a thick paste. Stir in chicken; reduce heat, and simmer 20 minutes.
- Stir rice and 2 cups water into tomato mixture. Cover and simmer 45 to 60 minutes, stirring gently once or twice (do not tear chicken). Remove from heat, and let stand at room temperature 30 minutes. Serve hot.

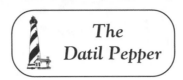
Fried Shrimp

6 pounds unpeeled, large fresh
   shrimp

6 large eggs, lightly beaten

1 (10-ounce) package cracker
   meal

1 pound shortening

⅔ cup mayonnaise

⅓ cup ketchup

½ teaspoon datil pepper sauce

- Peel shrimp, and devein. Dip each shrimp in egg, and dredge in cracker meal.
- Heat shortening to 375° in a large Dutch oven; add shrimp, and fry until golden brown. Drain on paper towels.
- Combine mayonnaise, ketchup, and pepper sauce in a small bowl, stirring well. Serve shrimp with pepper sauce.

Yield: 6 servings

Pasta

Basilica – Cathedral

This church was begun in 1793, financed largely by the Spanish royal treasury, plus contributions of material and labor on the part of the local citizens. The church was completed and dedicated in 1797 and became a cathedral in 1870. The bell tower and transept were added and the interior remodeled after a fire in 1887 destroyed all but the exterior walls.

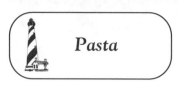

Pasta

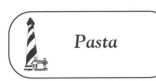
Pasta Primavera Gregory

½ pound spinach fettuccine, cooked

½ pound regular egg fettuccine, cooked

4 tablespoons salt

⅓ cup olive oil

½ cup chopped onion

¾ pound snow peas

⅓ pound sugar snap peas

¾ pound prosciutto, thinly sliced

2 red bell peppers, thinly sliced

2 Roma tomatoes

8 green onions, cut into ½-inch pieces

Salt and freshly ground pepper to taste

½ cup chopped fresh chives, basil, or other herb

¼ cup raspberry vinegar

¼ cup grated Parmesan cheese

1 cup pitted ripe olives

1 pound medium-size fresh shrimp, boiled and peeled

Grated zest of 1 orange, lemon, or lime

- Toss together first 5 ingredients in a large bowl.
- Arrange snow peas and snap peas in a steamer basket over boiling water; cover and steam several minutes or until crisp-tender. Plunge peas into ice water to stop the cooking process; let stand 10 minutes. Pat dry.
- Add peas, prosciutto, and next 5 ingredients to pasta mixture, tossing well. Sprinkle with vinegar, and toss gently. Add Parmesan cheese, and adjust seasonings to taste, tossing gently.
- Arrange pasta mixture on a serving platter. Sprinkle with olives, shrimp, and citrus zest. Serve at room temperature.

Yield: 8 servings

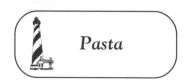
Macaroni and Cheese

1 tablespoon butter or margarine
1 tablespoon all-purpose flour
2 cups milk
2 cups (8 ounces) shredded sharp
  Cheddar cheese
Dash of salt
1 pinch of dry mustard
4 cups cooked macaroni
Breadcrumbs
Paprika to taste
Butter or margarine, cut up

- Melt 1 tablespoon butter in a medium saucepan over medium heat; add flour, stirring to make a paste. Gradually stir in milk and next 3 ingredients. Cook, stirring often, until cheese is melted.
- Layer one-third each of macaroni and cheese sauce in a butter 9 x 13 x 2-inch baking dish; repeat layers twice. Sprinkle with breadcrumbs and paprika; dot with butter.
- Bake at 300° for 1 hour.

Yield: 8 servings

Penne with Vodka and Spicy Cream Sauce

¼ cup extra-virgin olive oil
5 garlic cloves, minced
½ to ¾ teaspoon crushed red
  pepper flakes
1 pinch of salt
1 (28-ounce) can crushed
  tomatoes, pureed
1 pound penne pasta, cooked
2 tablespoons vodka
½ cup heavy cream
¼ cup chopped fresh Italian flat-
  leaf parsley

- Cook first 4 ingredients in a large skillet over medium heat 2 to 3 minutes or until garlic is golden. Stir in tomatoes; reduce heat, and simmer 15 minutes or until thickened. Add hot cooked pasta, tossing to coat. Add vodka, tossing to coat. Add cream, tossing to coat. Cover, reduce heat, and simmer 1 to 2 minutes. Add parsley, tossing to coat.

Yield: 6 to 8 servings

Serve this dish with Chianti Classico or a California red Zinfandel.

Red Bell Pepper Pesto

3 medium-size red bell peppers
½ cup grated Parmesan cheese
⅓ cup walnut pieces
1 garlic clove, minced
¼ teaspoon salt
¼ teaspoon pepper
⅓ cup light olive oil
Hot cooked angel hair pasta

- Bake bell peppers on a baking sheet at 500° for 20 minutes or until skin is blackened. Transfer peppers to a zip-top plastic bag; seal and chill 10 minutes or until cool. Peel peppers, discarding skin and seeds.
- Process peppers and next 5 ingredients in a food processor until smooth, stopping to scrape down sides. With machine running, add oil through food chute in a slow, steady stream. Process until well blended.
- Toss pesto with hot cooked pasta.

Yield: 6 servings

Bell peppers may be roasted and skinned ahead of time. Freeze until ready to use.

Marinara Sauce

3 tablespoons crushed garlic
1 tablespoon olive oil
½ cup chopped fresh oregano
1 cup chopped fresh parsley
5 tablespoons sugar
4 (28-ounce) cans crushed tomatoes
1 can water

- Sauté garlic in hot oil in a large saucepan until tender. Stir in oregano and next 4 ingredients. Bring to a boil. Reduce heat, and simmer 1 hour.

Yield: 6 to 8 servings

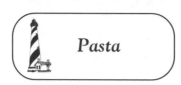

White Bean Pasta

4 garlic cloves, minced
⅛ cup olive oil
2 (14½-ounce) cans Italian-style diced tomatoes
¾ cup chopped fresh parsley, divided
1 (16-ounce) can white beans
¼ cup chopped pitted ripe olives
Ground pepper to taste
12 ounces regular or spinach fettuccine, cooked
1 cup crumbled feta cheese

• Sauté garlic in hot oil in a saucepan until tender; stir in tomatoes and ½ cup parsley. Reduce heat, and simmer 5 to 10 minutes or until thickened. Stir in beans and olives, and simmer 5 minutes. Stir in pepper.
• Arrange pasta in a serving bowl; top with sauce, and sprinkle with feta and remaining ¼ cup parsley.

Yield: 4 servings

Don't add salt to this recipe because the feta is salty. For a different dish, use a combination of spinach fettuccine and enriched angel hair pasta. Cook fettuccine first; drain and set aside. Cook angel hair; add fettuccine to angel hair, and cook 1 minute. Drain together; toss with sauce, and serve.

Pesto Sauce

2 handfuls fresh basil
1 to 2 tablespoons pine nuts
2 garlic cloves, chopped
3 tablespoons Parmesan cheese
1 cup olive oil
Salt and pepper to taste

• Process all ingredients in a food processor until smooth, stopping to scrape down sides. Cook in a saucepan over medium heat until thoroughly heated. Toss with hot cooked pasta.

Yield: 6 servings

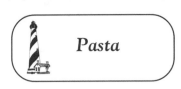
Chili Manicotti

2 tablespoons chopped onion

1 garlic clove, minced

1 tablespoon vegetable oil

1 (11¼-ounce) can condensed
   chili beef soup, undiluted

3 or 4 manicotti shells, cooked

½ cup (2 ounces) shredded sharp
   American cheese, divided

1 large egg, lightly beaten

¾ cup cream-style cottage cheese

2 tablespoons chopped green
   chiles

- Sauté onion and garlic in hot oil in a saucepan until tender; stir in soup.
- Cut pasta shells in half, if necessary, to fit into two individual baking dishes or a 6½ x 6½ x 2-inch baking dish. Combine ¼ cup cheese and next 3 ingredients; spoon evenly into shells.
- Pour half of soup mixture evenly into baking dishes; top evenly with stuffed shells. Pour remaining soup mixture evenly over shells, covering well.
- Bake, covered, at 350° for 35 to 40 minutes. Uncover and sprinkle with remaining ¼ cup cheese. Bake 2 to 3 more minutes. Remove from oven, and let stand at room temperature 5 minutes.

Yield: 2 servings

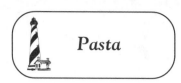

Mexican Lasagna

1½ pounds ground turkey

1 large onion, chopped

2 jalapeño peppers, chopped

Minced garlic to taste

2 (16-ounce) cans tomatoes

¼ teaspoon paprika

¼ teaspoon pepper

2 tablespoons chili powder

1 tablespoon ground cumin

1 can chopped pitted ripe olives

8 corn tortillas, halved

2 cups (8 ounces) ricotta cheese

1 large egg

2 cups (8 ounces) shredded
   Monterey Jack cheese

½ cup (2 ounces) shredded
   Cheddar cheese

- Cook first 4 ingredients in a large skillet over medium heat until turkey crumbles and is no longer pink. Break up tomatoes with a wooden spoon, and add to turkey mixture. Stir in paprika and next 4 ingredients. Bring to a boil; reduce heat, and simmer 10 minutes.
- Cook tortillas over medium-low heat in a small skillet coated with vegetable cooking spray until softened.
- Combine ricotta cheese and egg, stirring well.
- Spread one-third of meat mixture in a 9 x 13 x 2-inch baking dish; top with half each of Monterey Jack cheese and ricotta mixture. Top with half of tortillas, placing cut edges toward outside of dish. Repeat layers once. Top with remaining meat mixture. Sprinkle with Cheddar cheese.
- Bake at 350° for 25 to 35 minutes. Remove from oven, and let stand at room temperature 15 minutes.

Yield: 8 to 10 servings

Mediterranean Shrimp and Pasta

1 pound unpeeled, medium-size
    fresh shrimp
6 green onions, sliced
3 garlic cloves
2 tablespoons olive oil
1 (12-ounce) jar marinated
    artichoke hearts, undrained
6 Roma tomatoes, chopped
1 cup sliced fresh mushrooms
¼ cup dry white wine
2 teaspoons dried Italian
    seasoning
¼ teaspoon dried rosemary
¼ teaspoon salt
¼ teaspoon pepper
8 ounces angel hair pasta, cooked
Freshly grated Parmesan cheese

- Peel shrimp, and devein, if desired; set aside.
- Sauté green onions and garlic in hot oil in a large skillet over medium-high heat, stirring constantly, until tender. Stir in artichoke hearts and next 7 ingredients. Bring to a boil; reduce heat, and simmer 5 minutes. Add shrimp, and cook, stirring occasionally, 3 minutes or until shrimp turn pink.
- Serve shrimp mixture over hot cooked pasta, and sprinkle with cheese.

Yield: 4 servings

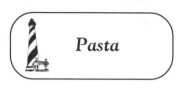

Stuffed Shells

1 package large pasta shells,
  uncooked

2 tablespoons olive oil

1 (15-ounce) container ricotta
  cheese

2 cups (8 ounces) shredded
  mozzarella cheese

1 cup grated Parmesan cheese

1 large egg

1 tablespoon garlic powder

Salt and pepper to taste

1 large jar tomato sauce

- Cook pasta shells and oil in boiling water to cover in a Dutch oven 10 minutes or until tender. Drain.
- Combine ricotta and next 5 ingredients; spoon 2 to 3 tablespoons mixture into each pasta shell, and place shells in an 8 x 8 x 2-inch baking dish. Pour tomato sauce over shells. Cover with aluminum foil.
- Bake at 350° for 1 hour.

Yield: 6 servings

Lasagna

½ pound ground beef

½ pound Italian sausage, with casings removed

½ pound lasagna noodles, uncooked

2 tablespoons olive oil

1 (15-ounce) container ricotta cheese

1 large egg

3 tablespoons dried oregano

1 tablespoon minced garlic

Salt and pepper to taste

1 large jar tomato sauce

2 cups (8 ounces) mozzarella cheese

1 cup grated Parmesan cheese

- Brown meats in a skillet over medium heat until they crumble and are no longer pink.
- Cook noodles and oil in boiling water to cover in a Dutch oven 15 minutes; drain.
- Combine ricotta cheese and egg in a bowl; stir in oregano, garlic, and salt and pepper to taste.
- Spread a small amount of tomato sauce in a 9 x 13 x 2-inch baking dish to cover bottom; layer with half each of noodles, meat, ricotta mixture, mozzarella cheese, and half of remaining sauce. Repeat layers once. Sprinkle with Parmesan cheese, and cover with aluminum foil.
- Bake at 350° for 45 minutes. Uncover and bake 15 more minutes.

Yield: 8 servings

This dish freezes well. To reheat, thaw in the refrigerator, and bake at 350° until thoroughly heated.

Linguine with Clam Sauce

8 ounces linguine, uncooked

1 tablespoon olive oil

½ cup white wine

¼ cup water

⅓ cup chopped shallots (2 large)

Minced garlic to taste

12 littleneck clams (optional)

1 (10-ounce) can baby clams,
    drained with juice reserved

1 teaspoon cornstarch

2 teaspoons water

1 cup buttermilk

2 tablespoons grated Parmesan
    cheese

1 teaspoon dried oregano

3 tablespoons chopped fresh or
    1 tablespoon dried basil

⅛ teaspoon pepper

1 tablespoon hot sauce

2 tablespoons chopped fresh or
    1 tablespoon dried parsley

- Cook linguine and oil in boiling water to cover in a Dutch oven 7 minutes or until tender; drain.
- Bring wine and next 3 ingredients to a boil in a saucepan; add fresh clams, if desired. Cover and cook until clams open; remove clams in their shells, and set aside. Add reserved clam juice to wine mixture, and cook until liquid is reduced by half. Reduce heat to low.
- Combine cornstarch and 2 teaspoons water, stirring well. Stir buttermilk and cornstarch mixture into wine mixture; cook 2 minutes or until thickened. Stir in Parmesan cheese, canned clams, oregano, and next 4 ingredients.
- Toss clam sauce and hot cooked pasta together in a serving bowl. Garnish with cooked clams in their shells.

Yield: 8 servings

Side Dishes

Castillo de San Marcos

The oldest building in St. Augustine—and its most popular tourist attraction—was begun in 1672 and finished in 1695 (with many later revisions).

The date of its beginning followed close on the heels of the British settlement of Charleston in 1670, which the Spanish saw as a threatening encroachment on their expansive definition of Florida. It continued as an active fort through the Spanish-American War of 1898.

Under the United States flag it was renamed Fort Marion, in honor of Francis Marion, the "Swamp Fox" of the American Revolution. The daughter of western warrior Geronimo was born here—and named Marion—when the fort was used as a prison for Apaches in the 1880s.

The coquina-stone Castillo was never taken in actual battle, but it was captured in the 1951 movie *Distant Drums*, starring Gary Cooper.

Potatoes & Rice

Vegetables

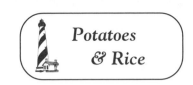

Red Beans and Rice with Ham Hocks and Smoked Sausage

1 pound dried red kidney beans

16 cups water, divided

4 ham hocks

2½ cups finely chopped celery

2 cups finely chopped onion

2 cups finely chopped green bell pepper

5 bay leaves

2½ teaspoons ground white pepper

2½ teaspoons dried thyme leaves

2 teaspoons garlic powder

2 teaspoons dried oregano leaves

1½ teaspoons ground red pepper

½ teaspoon ground black pepper

1 tablespoon hot sauce

1 pound smoked sausage, diagonally cut into ¼-inch slices

4½ cups hot cooked rice

- Soak beans in water 2 inches above beans; let stand overnight. Drain.
- Stir together 10 cups water and next 12 ingredients in a large Dutch oven; bring to a boil over high heat. Reduce heat, and simmer, stirring occasionally, 1½ hours or until meat is tender. Remove ham hocks, and set aside.
- Add beans and remaining 4 cups water to vegetable mixture; bring to a boil. Reduce heat, and simmer, stirring often, 30 minutes. Stir in sausage. Simmer 1 hour or until beans start breaking up. (If beans start to scorch, do not stir. Immediately remove from heat, and transfer to another pot without scraping any scorched beans into the mixture.) Return ham hocks to Dutch oven, and cook, stirring often, 30 minutes. Serve immediately over hot cooked rice.

Yield: 6 servings

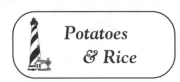

Petey's Rice

2 tablespoons butter or margarine
½ cup thinly sliced green onions
½ cup shredded carrot
1 cup apple or orange juice
1 cup water
1 cup uncooked long-grain rice
½ cup golden raisins
1 tablespoon brown sugar
½ teaspoon salt
½ teaspoon curry powder
¼ teaspoon pepper
¼ teaspoon ground cinnamon
¼ teaspoon ground ginger
¼ cup chopped cashews or
  peanuts
Garnish: thinly sliced green
  onions

• Melt butter in a medium
saucepan over medium heat; add
½ cup green onions and carrot,
and cook until crisp-tender. Stir
in apple juice and next 9
ingredients; bring to a boil.
Cover, reduce heat, and simmer
20 to 25 minutes or until rice is
tender and liquid is absorbed.
Stir in cashews just before
serving. Garnish, if desired.

Yield: 6 servings

St. Augustine Rice

½ cup butter or margarine
1 small onion, chopped
1 cup uncooked rice
1 can beef broth
1 small can mushrooms

• Melt butter in a skillet over
medium heat; add onion, and
sauté until browned. Remove
onion from skillet, reserving
drippings. Add rice to skillet,
and cook until browned.
• Combine onion, rice, broth, and
mushrooms in a baking dish.
• Bake at 325° for 15 to 20
minutes or until rice is tender.

Yield: 6 servings

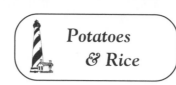
Mexican Party Rice

½ cup chopped red bell pepper

¼ cup chopped onion

1 garlic clove, minced

1 teaspoon vegetable oil

1¼ cups chicken broth

½ cup uncooked long-grain rice

½ cup frozen corn kernels, thawed

½ cup salsa

½ cup drained canned black beans

1 tablespoon chopped fresh cilantro

¼ teaspoon salt

Garnish: orange slices, fresh cilantro sprigs

• Cook first 3 ingredients in hot oil in a large saucepan coated with vegetable cooking spray over medium-high heat until crisp-tender. Add broth and next 3 ingredients; bring to a boil. Cover, reduce heat, and simmer 20 minutes. Remove from heat, and let stand 5 minutes or until liquid is absorbed. Stir in beans, chopped cilantro, and salt. Garnish, if desired.

Yield: 3 cups

Basic Fried Rice

1⅓ cups water, divided

1⅓ cups uncooked quick-cooking rice

3 tablespoons butter or margarine

1 large egg, lightly beaten

⅓ cup chopped onion

2 to 3 tablespoons soy sauce

• Bring 1 cup water to a boil; stir in rice. Remove from heat; cover and let stand 5 minutes.
• Melt butter in a 10-inch skillet over medium heat; add egg, and cook until set. Add cooked rice and onion; cook, stirring constantly, 5 minutes or until rice and onion are lightly browned.
• Combine remaining ⅓ cup water and soy sauce; stir into rice.

Yield: 4 servings (about 3 cups)

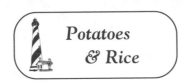
Soufflé Potatoes

6 large potatoes

4 teaspoons butter or margarine, melted

½ cup whipping cream

3 large eggs, separated

Salt and pepper to taste

- Preheat oven to 400°.
- Prick potatoes lightly with a fork, and bake at 400° for 1¼ hours or until tender. Slice a lid lengthwise off potatoes; scoop flesh into a bowl, reserving shells. Stir in butter and cream. Stir in yolks.
- Beat egg whites at medium speed with an electric mixer until stiff peaks form; fold into potato mixture. Season to taste with salt and pepper. Spoon potato mixture into reserved shells.
- Bake potatoes at 400° for 15 minutes or until soufflés are risen. Serve immediately.

Yield: 6 servings

With just a little extra work, you'll never eat plain baked potatoes again. Your regular baked potato will be transformed into a light and fluffy soufflé. This recipe is ideal with all meats, particularly steak.

Black Bean and Rice Salad

2⅔ cups chicken broth

1⅓ cups uncooked long-grain
rice

1 (16-ounce) can black beans,
rinsed and drained

¼ pound Roma tomatoes, seeded
and chopped

1 red bell pepper, chopped

1 cup chopped purple onion

¼ cup balsamic vinegar

3 tablespoons olive oil

2 tablespoons chopped fresh basil

1 tablespoons chopped garlic

Salt and pepper to taste

- Bring broth to a boil in a
saucepan; stir in rice. Cover,
reduce heat, and simmer 20
minutes or until rice is tender
and liquid is absorbed. Transfer
rice to a large bowl; let cool 15
minutes. Add beans and next 3
ingredients to rice, stirring well.
- Whisk together vinegar and next
3 ingredients; pour over rice
mixture, tossing to blend. Season
to taste with salt and pepper.
Serve warm or at room
temperature.

Yield: 8 servings

Rosemary Potatoes

1 garlic clove, minced

1½ teaspoons chopped fresh
rosemary

2 tablespoons olive oil

1½ pounds baking potatoes,
peeled and cubed

⅛ teaspoon salt

⅛ teaspoon freshly ground
pepper

Garnish: 2 to 3 fresh rosemary
sprigs

- Cook garlic and chopped
rosemary in hot oil in a large
skillet over medium heat 1 to
2 minutes. Stir in potato, salt,
and pepper; cook, stirring
occasionally, 5 minutes. Reduce
heat to medium-low, and cook
15 to 20 minutes, stirring often,
until crisp and brown. Garnish,
if desired.

Yield: 3 to 4 servings

Use new potatoes when available; cube them unpeeled.

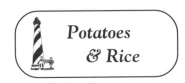

"I Love These" Potatoes

8 to 10 medium potatoes, peeled

1 (8-ounce) package cream cheese, softened

2 cups sour cream

⅓ cup chopped fresh chives

Salt and pepper to taste

¼ cup butter or margarine, cut up

Paprika to taste

- Boil potatoes in water to cover in a large Dutch oven until tender.
- Beat cream cheese and sour cream at medium speed with an electric mixer until smooth. Add potatoes, and beat until smooth. Stir in chives and salt and pepper to taste. Pour mixture into a greased 2-quart baking dish. Dot with butter, and sprinkle with paprika.
- Bake at 350° for 30 minutes.

Yield: 8 to 10 servings

This dish can be made ahead and baked when needed. This also makes really good leftovers.

Gigi's Potato Pancakes

1 pound potatoes, peeled

2 large eggs, lightly beaten

¼ cup finely chopped onion

1 teaspoon salt

¼ teaspoon pepper

2 to 4 tablespoons finely crushed saltine crackers

2 tablespoons vegetable oil

Toppings: sour cream, applesauce, brown sugar

- Coarsely shred potatoes into a large bowl of cold water; drain well. Combine potato and next 4 ingredients, stirring well. Stir in enough crushed crackers to make a thick batter.
- Cook ¼ cupfuls of batter in hot oil in a large skillet or on a griddle 5 minutes on each side or until brown and crisp. Drain on paper towels. Keep warm in a 200° oven.
- Serve pancakes hot with desired toppings.

Yield: 10 pancakes

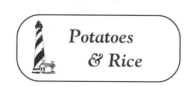

Scalloped Potatoes

8 to 9 red potatoes, unpeeled

1 cup milk

1 cup heavy cream

2 cups (8 ounces) shredded
   Cheddar cheese

1 teaspoon dry mustard

1½ teaspoons salt

½ teaspoon ground nutmeg

Dash of pepper

½ cup butter or margarine, cut
   up

Paprika to taste

- Boil potatoes in water to cover
  20 to 30 minutes or until tender.
- Cook milk and next 6
  ingredients in a saucepan over
  medium heat, stirring often,
  until cheese is melted (do not
  boil).
- Slice potatoes, and place them
  in a greased 9 x 13 x 2-inch
  baking dish; pour cheese sauce
  over top. Dot with butter, and
  sprinkle with paprika.
- Bake at 350° for 1 hour.

Yield: 8 servings

This dish can be prepared a day ahead and baked when ready.

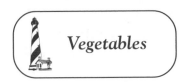

Sweet and Spicy Beans

1 (16-ounce) can black beans, rinsed and drained

1 (16-ounce) can black-eyed peas, rinsed and drained

1 (16-ounce) can red kidney beans, rinsed and drained

1 can corn, drained

1 (2-ounce) jar pimientos, chopped and drained

3 to 4 green onions, sliced

6 tablespoons red wine vinegar

6 tablespoons vegetable oil

6 tablespoons sugar

¾ to 1 teaspoon ground red pepper

¼ teaspoon salt

This recipe may be made ahead.

- Toss together first 6 ingredients in a large bowl.
- Whisk together vinegar and next 4 ingredients; pour over bean mixture. Chill 3 to 4 hours.

Yield: 8 to 10 servings

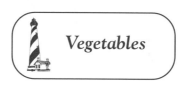

Glazed Carrots and Asparagus

1½ pounds small spring carrots, tops trimmed to 1 inch

1½ pounds asparagus tips, trimmed to 3 inches

2 tablespoons unsalted butter

Salt and freshly ground pepper to taste

- Cook carrots in boiling salted water in a large saucepan 5 minutes. Transfer to a plate and let cool. Add asparagus tips to boiling water and cook 3 minutes or just until tender. Drain asparagus and rinse with cold water. Cover and chill overnight, if desired.

- Melt 1 tablespoon butter in a skillet over medium heat; add carrots and cook until thoroughly heated. Season with salt and pepper to taste. Transfer to a plate; cover and keep warm. Melt remaining 1 tablespoon butter in skillet; add asparagus and cook until thoroughly heated. Season with salt and pepper to taste. Serve with carrots.

Yield: 8 servings

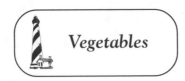

Vegetables

Broccoli with Lemon and Garlic

1 pound broccoli, trimmed and
    cut into spears
4 tablespoons butter or margarine
3 tablespoons lemon juice
1 garlic clove, minced

- Arrange broccoli in a steamer basket over boiling water; cover and steam 4 minutes or until crisp-tender. Arrange in a serving dish.
- Cook butter, lemon juice, and garlic in a small saucepan over medium-low heat, stirring often, until butter is melted. Pour over steamed broccoli; serve immediately.

Yield: 4 servings

Regal Broccoli

2 broccoli heads, cut into spears
2 egg whites, at room
    temperature
¼ teaspoon salt
⅓ cup mayonnaise
¼ cup freshly grated Parmesan
    cheese

- Preheat oven to 350°.
- Arrange broccoli in a steamer basket over boiling water; cover and steam 4 minutes or until crisp-tender. Arrange in a buttered quiche dish.
- Beat egg whites and salt at medium speed with an electric mixer until stiff peaks form; fold in mayonnaise. Spoon over broccoli. Sprinkle with Parmesan cheese.
- Bake at 350° for 15 minutes or until browned.

Yield: 6 servings

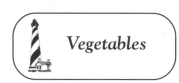
Okra and Tomatoes

½ pound bacon, diced
1½ tablespoons minced garlic
2 large onions, chopped
2 pounds okra, sliced
3 pounds tomatoes, chopped
2 tablespoons salt
1 tablespoon pepper
1½ tablespoons sugar
2 tablespoons minced fresh basil

• Cook bacon in a large skillet over medium heat until it begins to brown; add garlic and onion, and cook until tender. Add okra, and cook 5 minutes. Add tomato and next 4 ingredients, and cook 25 minutes or until tender.

Yield: 8 to 10 servings

Green Bean Salad with Basil Vinaigrette

2 pounds green beans, trimmed
3 shallots, minced
2 tablespoons balsamic or red
    wine vinegar
3 tablespoons olive or canola oil
⅔ cup chopped fresh basil
⅓ cup grated Romano cheese
Salt and pepper to taste

• Cook green beans in boiling salted water to cover in a large Dutch oven just until crisp-tender. Drain and rinse with cold water to stop the cooking process. Arrange in a serving dish.
• Combine shallots and vinegar in a bowl; gradually whisk in oil. Whisk in basil. Pour enough dressing over beans to coat; gently stir in cheese. Season with salt and pepper to taste.

Yield: 8 servings

This easy, quick recipe can be prepared ahead, but do not mix in cheese until ready to serve.

169

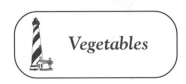
Raspberry Vinaigrette Asparagus

30 asparagus spears, trimmed to
4½ inches

1 (10-ounce) package frozen
raspberries in juice, thawed
and drained

⅓ cup olive oil

¼ cup whipping cream

2 tablespoons vinegar

¼ teaspoon salt

⅛ teaspoon ground black pepper

30 spinach leaves (about 3 cups),
stemmed

Garnishes: fresh raspberries,
chopped fresh chives, cracked
black pepper

- Bring 1 inch of water to a boil in
a Dutch oven; add asparagus,
and cook 3 to 4 minutes or until
crisp-tender. Drain and rinse
with cold water to stop the
cooking process.
- Puree thawed raspberries in a
food processor or blender; pour
through a wire-mesh strainer,
discarding seeds.
- Process oil and next 4
ingredients in a food processor or
blender until blended; add
raspberry puree, and process
until smooth.
- Arrange 5 spinach leaves on
each of 6 salad plates; arrange
5 asparagus spears on each bed of
spinach. Pour 2 tablespoons
raspberry vinaigrette over each
serving. Garnish, if desired.
Store leftover vinaigrette in the
refrigerator up to 7 days.

Yield: 6 servings

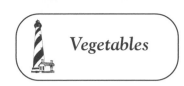
Squash and Tomato Bake

2 pounds yellow squash, sliced

1 cup water

2 (14½-ounce) cans stewed
    tomatoes, drained with ¼ cup
    liquid reserved

1 tablespoon all-purpose flour

2 teaspoons sugar

1 teaspoon salt

1 teaspoon paprika

½ teaspoon garlic powder

⅛ teaspoon pepper

⅛ teaspoon dried basil

2 cups (8 ounces) shredded
    mozzarella cheese

½ cup grated Parmesan cheese

- Bring squash and 1 cup water to a boil in a large saucepan; cover, reduce heat, and simmer, stirring occasionally, 10 minutes or until tender. Remove from heat; drain.
- Bring tomatoes, reserved tomato liquid, and next 7 ingredients to a boil in a small saucepan; reduce heat, and simmer 5 minutes. Remove from heat.
- Place half of squash in a shallow 2-quart baking dish; pour one-fourth of tomato mixture over squash. Top with 1 cup mozzarella and one-fourth of tomato mixture. Repeat layers with remaining squash, tomato mixture, and mozzarella cheese. Sprinkle with Parmesan cheese.
- Bake at 350° for 30 minutes. Remove from oven, and let stand 10 minutes before serving.

Yield: 6 to 8 servings

Parmesan cheese may be sprinkled over casserole during last 5 minutes of baking time, if desired. (Top will not be crusty.)

Carrot Soufflé

1 pound carrots, sliced
½ cup butter or margarine, melted
1 teaspoon baking powder
1 cup sugar
1 teaspoon vanilla extract
2 tablespoons all-purpose flour
3 large eggs

• Arrange carrot slices in a steamer basket over boiling water; cover and steam 8 to 10 minutes or until tender; drain. Process carrots and next 6 ingredients in a food processor or blender until smooth. Pour into a buttered baking dish.
• Bake at 350° for 45 minutes.

Yield: 6 servings

St. Augustine Sweet Onion Pie

3 tablespoons butter or margarine
1 tablespoon olive oil
4 St. Augustine sweet onions, thinly sliced
2 large eggs
1 cup half-and-half
2 tablespoons all-purpose flour
1 teaspoon salt
⅛ teaspoon pepper
1 pinch of ground nutmeg
¼ cup (2 ounces) shredded Swiss cheese
1 partially baked 9-inch pastry shell
Garnish: chopped fresh parsley

• Melt butter and oil in a skillet over low heat; add onion, and sauté until golden.
• Whisk together eggs and next 5 ingredients; stir in onion and half of cheese. Pour into pastry shell, and sprinkle with remaining half of cheese.
• Bake at 375° for 25 to 30 minutes or until golden brown. Garnish, if desired.

Yield: 4 servings

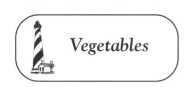
Scalloped St. Augustine Sweet Onions

¼ cup butter or margarine

3 medium St. Augustine sweet
    onions, sliced

¼ cup chopped green bell pepper

2 tablespoons chopped pimiento

1 cup (4 ounces) shredded Swiss
    cheese

1 cup cracker crumbs, divided

2 large eggs

¾ cup half-and-half

1 teaspoon salt

⅛ teaspoon pepper

2 tablespoons butter or
    margarine, melted

- Melt ¼ cup butter in a saucepan over medium heat; add onion and bell pepper, and sauté until tender. Stir in pimiento. Place half of onion mixture in a greased baking dish; sprinkle with ½ cup cheese and ½ cup cracker crumbs. Top with remaining half of onion mixture and ½ cup cheese.
- Whisk together eggs and next 3 ingredients; pour over casserole.
- Combine remaining ½ cup cracker crumbs and 2 tablespoons melted butter; sprinkle over casserole.
- Bake at 325° for 25 minutes or until set. Serve hot.

Yield: 6 to 10 servings

This recipe may be prepared a day ahead; do not bake, and chill over-night. Bake when ready to serve.

Spinach Casserole

3 (8-ounce) packages frozen
  chopped spinach, cooked and
  well drained
1½ cups (6 ounces) shredded
  Cheddar or mozzarella cheese
1½ cups low-fat cottage cheese
2 large eggs, lightly beaten
1 cup chopped Vidalia sweet
  onion
1 tablespoon all-purpose flour
Salt and pepper to taste
Freshly grated Parmesan cheese

- Combine first 7 ingredients,
  stirring well. Spoon into a
  baking dish.
- Bake at 350° for 30 minutes.
  Sprinkle with Parmesan cheese,
  and bake 3 minutes.

Yield: 8 servings

Spinach-Artichoke Casserole

½ stick butter or margarine
½ cup chopped onion
3 (10-ounce) packages frozen
  chopped spinach, cooked and
  well drained
2 (16-ounce) cans artichoke
  hearts, cut into fourths
2 cups sour cream
Salt and pepper to taste
½ cup grated Parmesan cheese

- Melt butter in a skillet over
  medium heat; add onion, and
  sauté until tender. Combine
  onion, spinach, and next 3
  ingredients; stir in ¼ cup cheese.
  Spoon into a 2½-quart baking
  dish, and sprinkle with
  remaining ¼ cup cheese.
- Bake at 350° for 25 to 30
  minutes.

Yield: 8 servings

Light sour cream may be substituted for regular, if desired.

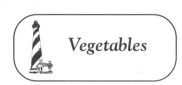
Champignons a la Crème

4 teaspoons unsalted butter

1 pound fresh button
mushrooms, stalks trimmed to
caps

Salt and pepper to taste

Dried mixed herbs to taste

1 tablespoon all-purpose flour

½ cup whipping cream

1 rounded tablespoon chopped
fresh parsley

2 tablespoons lemon juice

• Melt butter in a skillet over medium heat; add mushrooms, and sauté 2 to 3 minutes, tossing well. Season to taste with salt, pepper, and herbs. Cook 2 to 3 more minutes. Sprinkle with flour, stirring with a wooden spoon to blend. Gradually stir in cream, and bring to a boil, stirring constantly; boil, stirring constantly, until thickened. Reduce heat, and simmer 1 to 2 minutes. Stir in parsley and lemon juice, and serve immediately.

Yield: 4 servings

*Choose small, firm mushrooms so they will not break up during cooking.
This recipe is wonderful served with grilled steak or chicken.*

Stuffed Tomatoes

8 medium-size firm tomatoes

1 cup Italian-seasoned
breadcrumbs

⅓ cup chopped green onions

¼ cup chopped fresh thyme

2 garlic cloves

½ teaspoon salt

½ teaspoon pepper

¼ cup olive oil

• Cut a ¼-inch slice from the top of each tomato; scoop out pulp, reserving pulp. Place shells upside down to drain.
• Combine pulp, breadcrumbs, and next 6 ingredients, stirring well; spoon into tomato shells. Place tomatoes into a 9 x 13 x 2-inch baking dish.
• Bake at 450° for 10 minutes. Serve whole, or cut each in half.

Yield: 8 or 16 servings

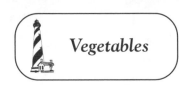
Crusty Topped Cauliflower

1 large cauliflower
½ cup mayonnaise
2 teaspoons Dijon mustard
½ to ¾ cup (4 to 6 ounces) shredded Cheddar cheese

- Cook cauliflower in a small amount of boiling salted water in a Dutch oven 20 minutes; drain carefully. Transfer cauliflower to a flat pan. Combine mayonnaise and mustard; spread over cauliflower. Sprinkle with cheese.
- Bake at 350° for 10 minutes or until cheese is melted.

Yield: 6 servings

Eggplant Casserole

1 large eggplant, peeled and diced
2½ cups torn pieces of bread
⅛ teaspoon salt
1 tablespoon chopped fresh parsley
1 tablespoon minced onion
1 large egg, lightly beaten
1 tablespoon butter or margarine
¼ cup (2 ounces) shredded Cheddar cheese

- Arrange eggplant in a steamer basket over boiling water; cover and steam 8 to 10 minutes or until crisp-tender. Combine bread and next 5 ingredients, stirring well; add eggplant, tossing gently. Pour into a greased 1-quart baking dish. Sprinkle with cheese.
- Bake at 350° for 20 minutes.

Yield: 4 servings

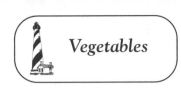
Mom's Corn Pudding

4 large eggs

1 cup sugar

2 tablespoons all-purpose flour

½ teaspoon salt

1 cup milk

1 small can evaporated milk

3 tablespoons butter or
    margarine, melted

1 large can cream-style corn

1 small can cream-style corn

- Combine all ingredients, stirring well. Pour into a 9 x 13 x 2-inch baking dish.
- Bake at 350° for 45 minutes.

Yield: 8 to 12 servings

Casserole Carrots

2 pounds carrots, sliced
    diagonally

2 tablespoons butter or
    margarine

2 tablespoons all-purpose flour

¾ teaspoon dry mustard

½ teaspoon salt

¼ teaspoon paprika

⅛ teaspoon pepper

2 cups milk

¼ cup grated Parmesan cheese

½ cup canned French fried
    onions

- Cook carrot slices in boiling salted water 20 minutes or until tender; drain.
- Melt butter in a saucepan over medium heat; add flour and next 4 ingredients, stirring until smooth. Add milk, and cook, stirring constantly, until thickened and bubbly. Stir in cheese. Stir in carrot slices, and spoon into a 1½-quart baking dish.
- Bake, covered, at 350° for 30 minutes. Uncover and sprinkle with fried onions; bake, uncovered, 3 to 5 minutes.

Yield: 8 servings

177

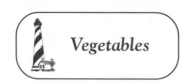

Lima Beans with Gingersnap Casserole

2 packages frozen lima beans, thawed

1 cup sour cream

2 tablespoons brown sugar

1 tablespoon prepared mustard

Dash of Worcestershire sauce

1¼ cups crushed gingersnaps

¼ cup sweet butter, melted

- Combine first 5 ingredients; spoon into a baking dish. Combine gingersnaps and butter, and sprinkle over casserole.
- Bake at 350° for 45 minutes.

Yield: 6 servings

Bourbon Sweet Potatoes

4 pounds sweet potatoes

½ cup butter or margarine, softened

½ cup bourbon

⅓ cup orange juice

¼ cup firmly packed light brown sugar

1 teaspoon salt

½ teaspoon apple pie spice

⅓ cup pecans, chopped

- Preheat oven to 350°.
- Cook potatoes in boiling salted water to cover in a large Dutch oven until tender. Drain potatoes; peel and mash. Beat mashed potato and next 6 ingredients at medium speed with an electric mixer until blended. Spoon into a greased 9 x 13 x 2-inch baking dish. Sprinkle with pecans.
- Bake at 350° for 45 minutes.

Yield: 8 servings

Desserts

Alcazar Hotel

Flagler-era St. Augustine was to have four monumental hotels built around a landscaped plaza. The Alcazar was one of these, constructed soon after the flagship Ponce de Leon Hotel across the street.

Like the Ponce, it was designed by architects Carrere and Hastings and built by contractors McGuire and McDonald. At the last minute, Henry Flagler was seized with cheapness and decided not to build the grand colonnade designed for the front of the building, leaving that facade always looking rather naked.

The back part of the building housed the popular casino and the indoor swimming pool. Gertrude Ederle swam there in the 1920s, shortly before gaining fame as the first woman to swim the English Channel.

The Alcazar closed during the Depression of the 1930s, reopening after World War II as the Lightner Museum—sometimes called "The Smithsonian of the South." In later decades it shared the use of the building with St. Augustine's City Hall.

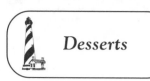

Desserts

Cakes

Pies

Cookies

Other Desserts

Almost Lindy's Cheesecake

1 package graham cracker
 crumbs

5 (8-ounce) packages cream
 cheese, softened

1¾ cups sugar

3 tablespoons all-purpose flour

5 medium eggs

2 egg yolks

1½ teaspoons grated lemon rind

½ teaspoon vanilla extract

¼ cup heavy cream

- Prepare graham cracker crust in a 9-inch springform pan according to package directions.
- Preheat oven to 475°.
- Beat cream cheese, sugar, and flour at medium speed with an electric mixer until smooth. Add eggs and egg yolks, 1 at a time, beating well after each addition. Add lemon rind, vanilla, and cream, beating well. Pour into prepared crust.
- Bake at 475° for 10 minutes. Reduce oven temperature to 200°, and bake 1 hour. Turn oven off, and do not open oven door. Let stand in oven 1 hour. Partially open oven door, and let stand in oven 30 minutes. Let cool on a wire rack. Chill. Top with strawberries, if desired.

Yield: 12 servings

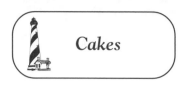

Mocha Mousse Cheesecake

½ cup unsalted butter, melted

2 cups cream-filled chocolate
sandwich cookie crumbs

3 (8-ounce) packages cream
cheese

1 cup sugar

2 large eggs

8 (1-ounce) semisweet chocolate
baking squares, melted and
cooled

¾ cup sour cream

7 tablespoons strong brewed
coffee

2 tablespoons heavy cream

3 tablespoons rum

- Preheat oven to 350°.
- Combine butter and cookie
  crumbs; press into the bottom
  and up the sides of an 8-inch
  springform pan.
- Process cream cheese, sugar, and
  eggs in a blender until smooth;
  add melted chocolate and next
  4 ingredients, and process until
  well blended. Pour into prepared
  crust.
- Bake at 350° for 45 minutes.
  Turn oven off, and partially
  open oven door; let stand in
  oven 1 hour. Chill overnight on
  a wire rack.

Yield: 12 servings

White Chocolate-Raspberry Cheesecake

1½ cups zwieback crumbs

1 cup toasted almonds, ground

4½ tablespoons butter or margarine, melted

4 (1-ounce) white chocolate baking squares

2 (8-ounce) packages cream cheese, softened

⅔ cup sugar

2 teaspoons vanilla extract

¾ teaspoon grated lemon rind

2 large eggs

1 quart raspberries, divided

1 (8-ounce) container sour cream

2 tablespoons sugar

1 teaspoon vanilla extract

½ cup seedless raspberry jam, melted

- Combine first 3 ingredients; press into the bottom and up the sides of an aluminum foil-lined 8-inch springform pan.
- Bake at 350° for 10 minutes.
- Place chocolate in the top of a double boiler; bring water to a boil. Cook, stirring constantly, until chocolate is melted.
- Beat cream cheese and next 3 ingredients at medium speed with an electric mixer until smooth; add eggs, 1 at a time, beating well after each addition. Beat in melted chocolate. Pour half of batter into prepared crust; sprinkle ¾ quart raspberries over top. Pour remaining batter over raspberries.
- Bake at 350° for 45 minutes.
- Combine sour cream, 2 tablespoons sugar, and vanilla; spread over cake. Bake 5 minutes. Let cool on a wire rack.
- Sprinkle ¼ quart raspberries over cheesecake; pour melted jam over berries. Chill.

Yield: 8 servings

This recipe sounds more complicated than it is. The recipe easily doubles, and it can be frozen without the raspberry and jam topping. Zwieback and almonds can be processed together in a blender or food processor.

Key Lime Cheesecake

1¼ cups graham cracker crumbs

6 tablespoons unsalted butter, softened

2 tablespoons sugar

1 (8-ounce) package cream cheese, softened

1 (14-ounce) can sweetened condensed milk

½ cup fresh Key lime juice

1 tablespoon vanilla extract

1 cup frozen whipped topping, thawed

Garnish: key lime twists, whipped topping rosettes

- Preheat oven to 350°.
- Combine first 3 ingredients; press into the bottom and up the sides of a 9-inch springform pan.
- Bake at 350° for 10 minutes. Let cool.
- Beat cream cheese and condensed milk at medium speed with an electric mixer until creamy; add lime juice, vanilla, and 1 cup whipped topping, beating well. Pour into prepared crust. Chill 3 hours or overnight. Garnish, if desired.

Yield: 8 servings

To make whipped topping rosettes, spoon whipped topping into a piping bag fitted with a rosette tip. Pipe whirls around the edge of the cheese-cake.

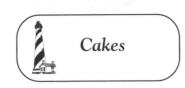
Chop Suey Cake

2 cups all-purpose flour

2 teaspoons baking soda

2 cups sugar

2 large eggs

1 large can crushed pineapple in juice

1 cup chopped nuts

2 tablespoons ground cinnamon

2 tablespoons pumpkin pie spice

1 (8-ounce) package cream cheese, softened

½ cup butter or margarine, softened

2 cups powdered sugar

1 teaspoon vanilla extract

This cake freezes beautifully.

- Combine first 8 ingredients, stirring well. Pour into a 9 x 13 x 2-inch pan coated with vegetable cooking spray.
- Bake at 350° for 35 to 40 minutes.
- Beat cream cheese and next 3 ingredients at medium speed with an electric mixer until creamy; pour over hot cake. Let cool.

Yield: 12 servings

Maureen's English Fruit Cake

1 cup shortening

2 cups firmly packed brown sugar

4 large eggs

3 cups all-purpose flour

1 teaspoon baking powder

1 teaspoon salt

1 teaspoon ground cinnamon

1 teaspoon ground allspice

½ teaspoon ground nutmeg

½ teaspoon ground cloves

¾ cup grape juice

3½ cups candied fruit

1¼ cups dark raisins (8 ounces)

1¼ cups golden raisins (8 ounces)

2 cups walnuts (4 ounces)

1 (4-ounce) package dates

- Beat first 3 ingredients at medium speed with an electric mixer until creamy.
- Sift together flour and next 6 ingredients; add to creamed mixture alternately with grape juice, beginning and ending with flour mixture and beating well after each addition.
- Combine candied fruit and next 4 ingredients in a large bowl; pour batter over fruit mixture, stirring well. Pour into 2 paper-lined 5 x 9-inch loaf pans.
- Bake at 275° for 3 to 3½ hours with 2 cups water in a pan on bottom shelf of oven.

Yield: 2 loaves

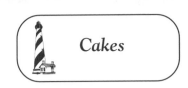

Quick Cinnamon Cake

2 cups all-purpose flour

2 teaspoons baking powder

1 teaspoon salt

⅓ cup shortening

1 cup sugar

2 large eggs, lightly beaten

¾ cup milk

1 teaspoon vanilla extract

½ cup butter or margarine, melted

3 tablespoons sugar

1 tablespoon ground cinnamon

- Sift together first 3 ingredients.
- Beat shortening and 1 cup sugar at medium speed with an electric mixer until creamy; add eggs, beating well. Add flour mixture alternately with milk and vanilla, beginning and ending with flour mixture and beating well after each addition. Pour batter into a greased 9 x 13 x 2-inch pan. Pour melted butter over top.
- Combine 3 tablespoons sugar and cinnamon; sprinkle over cake.
- Bake at 375° for 30 minutes.

Yield: 8 servings

For a variation stir ½ cup chopped nuts or ⅓ cup red cinnamon candies into batter. Children love this cake.

Sour Cream Coffee Cake

¾ cup California walnuts, finely
  chopped

1½ teaspoons ground cinnamon

2 cups sugar, divided

¾ cup butter or margarine

3 cups all-purpose flour

1½ teaspoons double-acting
  baking powder

1½ teaspoons baking soda

1½ cups sour cream

3 large eggs

1½ teaspoons vanilla extract

- Combine walnuts, cinnamon, and ¾ cup sugar in a bowl; set aside.
- Beat butter and remaining 1¼ cups sugar at medium speed with an electric mixer until light and fluffy. Add flour and next 5 ingredients, beating at low speed until blended and scraping sides of bowl. Increase speed to medium, and beat 3 minutes.
- Preheat oven to 350°.
- Spread half of batter in a greased 10-inch tube pan; sprinkle with half of nut mixture. Spread with remaining batter, and sprinkle with remaining nut mixture.
- Bake at 350° for 1 hour to 1 hour and 5 minutes or until cake pulls from sides of pan. Let cool on a wire rack.

Yield: 12 servings

Chocolate Whatever

1 (18.25-ounce) package
   chocolate cake mix
2 large packages chocolate
   pudding mix
Chopped English toffee candy
   bars
Frozen whipped topping, thawed

- Bake cake in a 9 x 13 x 2-inch pan according to package directions. Let cool, and break into chunks.
- Prepare pudding according to package directions.
- Layer one-third each of cake chunks, pudding, candy bar pieces, and whipped topping in a large trifle or serving bowl. Repeat layers twice using remaining ingredients and ending with whipped topping. Chill.

Yield: 10 servings

From age 8 to 80 everybody loves this dessert.

Robin's Famous Pound Cake

1 cup butter, softened
2½ cups sugar
6 large eggs
3 cups all-purpose flour
1 cup whipping cream
½ teaspoon vanilla extract

- Beat butter and sugar at medium speed with an electric mixer until creamy; add eggs, 1 at a time, beating well after each addition. Add flour and cream alternately, beginning and ending with flour and beating well after each addition. Stir in vanilla. Pour batter into a greased 10-inch tube pan.
- Bake at 300° for 1½ hours.

Yield: 12 servings

Heath Bar Coffee Cake

2 cups firmly packed brown
  sugar
2 cups all-purpose flour
½ cup butter or margarine,
  chilled and cut up
1 large egg, lightly beaten
1 teaspoon baking soda
1 pinch of salt
1 teaspoon vanilla extract
3 double English toffee candy
  bars, chopped
½ cup chopped nuts

- Combine sugar and flour in a large bowl; cut in butter with a pastry blender until mixture is crumbly. Reserve 1 cup butter mixture.
- Add egg and next 3 ingredients to remaining flour mixture, stirring until smooth. Pour batter in a greased 9 x 13 x 2-inch pan. Sprinkle with reserved butter mixture.
- Combine candy bar pieces and nuts; sprinkle over batter.
- Bake at 350° for 25 to 30 minutes.

Yield: 8 servings

Sour Cream Pound Cake

1 cup butter, softened
3 cups sugar
1 teaspoon vanilla extract
1 cup sour cream
6 large eggs
3 cups cake flour
¼ teaspoon baking soda
¼ teaspoon baking powder

- Beat butter at medium speed with an electric mixer until creamy; add sugar, vanilla, and sour cream, beating until creamy. Add eggs, 1 at a time, beating well after each addition.
- Sift together flour, soda, and baking powder; add to creamed mixture, beating well. Pour batter into a greased 10-inch tube pan.
- Bake at 325° for 1½ hours or until done.

Yield: 12 servings

Chocolate Pound Cake

1½ cups butter, softened
3 cups sugar
5 large eggs
3 cups all-purpose flour
½ teaspoon baking powder
¼ teaspoon salt
4 tablespoons cocoa
1 cup milk
1 teaspoon vanilla extract
Chocolate Icing

- Beat butter and sugar at medium speed with an electric mixer until creamy; add eggs, 1 at a time, beating well after each addition.
- Sift together flour and next 3 ingredients; add to creamed mixture alternately with milk and vanilla, beginning and ending with flour mixture and beating well after each addition. Pour batter into a greased 10-inch tube pan.
- Bake at 325° for 1½ hours. Remove from oven, and let cool on a wire rack. Remove cake from pan, and drizzle with Chocolate Icing.

Chocolate Icing
½ cup butter or margarine
3 teaspoons cocoa
¼ cup evaporated milk
¾ to 1 (16-ounce) package powdered sugar
1 teaspoon vanilla extract

- Cook all ingredients in a saucepan over low heat, stirring constantly, until thickened.

Yield: 12 servings

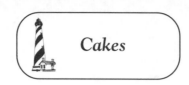

Fabulous Peach Torte

70 vanilla wafers, crushed (about 2½ cups)

⅓ cup butter or margarine, softened

½ cup cold water

2 cups heavy cream

2 tablespoons sugar

¼ teaspoon almond extract

3 large peaches, peeled and sliced or 1 (16-ounce) can peaches, sliced in half lengthwise

• Preheat oven to 375°.

• Cut 3 (8-inch) wax paper circles, and place on a large baking sheet.

• Beat wafer crumbs and butter at medium speed with an electric mixer until crumbly; gradually stir in ½ cup cold water until a moist dough forms. Divide dough into thirds. Press each portion onto a wax paper circle.

• Bake at 375° for 12 to 15 minutes. Let cool 15 minutes or until firm.

• Beat cream, sugar, and almond extract at medium speed with an electric mixer until stiff peaks form. Reserve 8 peach slices for garnish. Chop remaining peaches, and fold into cream mixture.

• Remove wax paper from crust rounds; spread 1 round with one-third of peach mixture. Top with 1 round, and spread with half of remaining peach mixture. Top with remaining round, and spread with remaining peach mixture. Chill 4 to 6 hours.

Yield: 8 servings

Carrot Cake

1 cup sugar
¾ cup vegetable oil
1½ cups all-purpose flour
1½ teaspoons baking powder
1 teaspoon ground cinnamon
½ teaspoon salt
2 large eggs
2 cups shredded carrot
1 cup raisins
1 cup chopped walnuts
Cream Cheese Frosting

Cream Cheese Frosting
1 (3-ounce) package cream
  cheese, softened
¼ cup butter or margarine,
  softened
1 teaspoon vanilla extract
2 cups powdered sugar

- Beat sugar and oil at medium speed with an electric mixer until creamy; add flour and next 3 ingredients, beating well. Add eggs, 1 at a time, beating well after each addition. Stir in carrot, raisins, and walnuts. Pour batter into a greased 9 x 13 x 2-inch pan.
- Bake at 350° for 45 to 50 minutes. Let cool on a wire rack. Spread with Cream Cheese Frosting.

- Beat first 3 ingredients at medium speed with an electric mixer until creamy; add sugar, beating until smooth.

Yield: 10 servings

Anke's German Chocolate Cake

1 (4-ounce) package sweet
  baking chocolate

½ cup boiling water

1 cup butter or margarine,
  softened

2 cups sugar

4 large eggs, separated

1 teaspoon vanilla extract

2½ cups all-purpose flour

1 teaspoon baking soda

½ teaspoon salt

1 cup buttermilk

Coconut-Pecan Frosting

- Combine chocolate and ½ cup boiling water in a small bowl, stirring until chocolate is melted. Let cool.
- Beat butter and sugar at medium speed with an electric mixer until creamy; add egg yolks, 1 at a time, beating well after each addition. Add melted chocolate and vanilla, beating well.
- Sift together flour, soda, and salt; add to creamed mixture alternately with buttermilk, beginning and ending with flour mixture and beating well after each addition.
- Beat egg whites at medium speed with an electric mixer until soft peaks form; fold into batter. Pour batter into 3 wax paper-lined 8- or 9-inch round cake pans.
- Bake at 350° for 30 to 40 minutes. Let cool, and remove from pans. Spread Coconut-Pecan Frosting on top of each layer, and stack layers.

Coconut-Pecan Frosting

1 cup evaporated milk

1 cup sugar

3 egg yolks, lightly beaten

½ cup butter or margarine

1 teaspoon vanilla extract

1½ cups flaked coconut

1 cup chopped pecans

- Cook first 5 ingredients in a saucepan over medium heat, stirring constantly, 12 minutes or until thickened. Let cool until spreading consistency.

Yield: 12 servings

Mrs. Apelt's Sheet Cake

2 cups sugar
2 cups all-purpose flour
1½ teaspoons salt, divided
½ cup butter or margarine
4 tablespoons cocoa
½ cup vegetable oil
1 cup water
2 large eggs, lightly beaten
½ cup buttermilk
1 teaspoon vanilla extract
Chocolate-Buttermilk Icing

Chocolate-Buttermilk Icing
½ cup butter or margarine
3 tablespoons cocoa
6 tablespoons buttermilk
1 teaspoon vanilla
1 (16-ounce) package powdered
   sugar

• Combine sugar, flour, and ½ teaspoon salt in a large bowl.
• Bring butter and next 3 ingredients to a boil in a saucepan; add to flour mixture, stirring well. Stir in remaining 1 teaspoon salt, eggs, buttermilk, and vanilla. Pour batter into a greased 10½ x 15 x 1-inch jelly-roll pan.
• Bake at 350° for 20 minutes. Remove from oven, and pour Chocolate-Buttermilk Icing over warm cake.

• Beat first 4 ingredients at medium speed with an electric mixer until creamy; gradually add powdered sugar, beating well.

Yield: 12 servings

Betty's Coconut-Sour Cream Cake

1 (18.25-ounce) package yellow
cake mix

1 (16-ounce) container sour
cream

2 cups sugar

1 (18-ounce) package frozen
coconut, thawed and divided

1 (8-ounce) container frozen
whipped topping, thawed

- Bake cake in 2 (8-inch) round
cake pans according to package
directions. Let cool, and slice
each into 2 layers.
- Combine sour cream, sugar, and
12 ounces coconut in a bowl.
Combine 1 cup coconut mixture
and whipped topping in a
separate bowl.
- Spoon remaining coconut-sour
cream mixture evenly on cut
sides of layers. Stack layers; ice
top and sides of cake with
whipped topping mixture. Cover
and chill 3 days.
- Pat remaining 6 ounces coconut
on top and sides of cake before
serving.

Yield: 10 servings

This cake must chill 3 days before serving.

Oatmeal Cake
with Broiled Coconut Topping

1½ cups boiling water
1 cup quick-cooking rolled oats
1½ cups sifted all-purpose flour
1 teaspoon baking soda
1 teaspoon salt
1 teaspoon ground cinnamon
½ teaspoon baking powder
½ cup butter or margarine,
  softened
1 cup granulated sugar
1 cup firmly packed light brown
  sugar
2 large eggs
Coconut Topping

- Preheat oven to 350°.
- Combine 1½ cups boiling water and oats; set aside.
Sift together flour and next 4 ingredients.
- Beat butter and sugars at medium speed with an electric mixer until mealy; add eggs, 1 at a time, beating until light and fluffy. Stir in oats; add flour mixture, beating well. Pour batter into a greased and floured 9-inch square pan.
- Bake at 350° for 40 minutes. Let cool in pan 10 minutes. Transfer cake to a baking sheet, and cool completely. Spread Coconut Topping over cake. Broil 2 to 3 minutes or until topping is lightly browned.

Coconut Topping
1⅓ cups flaked coconut
¼ cup butter or margarine,
  melted
½ cup firmly packed brown sugar
¼ cup heavy cream or milk
1 teaspoon vanilla

- Combine all ingredients in a bowl.

Yield: 8 servings

Pumpkin Cake

3 cups all-purpose flour

2 tablespoons baking powder

2 teaspoons baking soda

1 teaspoon salt

3 teaspoons ground cinnamon

1 teaspoon ground nutmeg

4 large eggs, lightly beaten

2 cups sugar

2 cups canned or cooked and
   mashed pumpkin

1¼ cups vegetable oil

Cream Cheese Icing

Cream Cheese Icing

1 (8-ounce) package cream
   cheese, softened

½ cup butter or margarine,
   softened

1 (16-ounce) package powdered
   sugar, sifted

2 teaspoons vanilla extract

1 cup chopped pecans

• Preheat oven to 350°.

• Sift together first 6 ingredients
  twice.

• Beat eggs and sugar at medium
  speed with an electric mixer until
  creamy; add pumpkin and oil,
  beating well. Add flour mixture,
  beating well. Spoon batter into a
  greased and floured 10-inch tube
  pan or 2 (5 x 9-inch) loaf pans.

• Bake at 350° for 1 hour (tube
  pan) or 50 minutes (loaf pans).
  Let cool, and remove from pans.
  Spread with Cream Cheese
  Icing.

• Beat cream cheese and butter at
  medium speed with an electric
  mixer until creamy; add
  powdered sugar, one-fourth at a
  time, beating well. Stir in
  vanilla. Stir in nuts.

Yield: 12 servings

Chocolate Eclair Cake

2 small packages French vanilla
  instant pudding mix
3½ cups milk
1 (8-ounce) container frozen
  whipped topping, thawed
1 (16-ounce) package graham
  crackers
Chocolate Frosting

- Beat pudding and milk at medium speed with an electric mixer 2 minutes; fold whipped topping into pudding.
- Place a single layer of graham crackers in a greased 9 x 13 x 2-inch pan. Pour half of pudding mixture over graham crackers; repeat layers once. Top with a third layer of graham crackers. Chill at least 2 hours.
- Spread Chocolate Frosting over top of dessert. Chill at least 24 hours.

Chocolate Frosting
2 (1-ounce) chocolate baking
  squares, melted
2 teaspoons light corn syrup
2 teaspoons vanilla extract
3 tablespoons milk
1½ cups powdered sugar

- Beat all ingredients at medium speed with an electric mixer until smooth.

Yield: 12 servings

Chocolate Sheath Cake

2 cups sugar
2 cups all-purpose flour
1 teaspoon baking soda
1 teaspoon ground cinnamon
1 cup water
½ cup butter or margarine
½ cup vegetable oil
¼ cup cocoa
½ cup buttermilk
2 large eggs, lightly beaten
1 teaspoon vanilla extract
Chocolate-Pecan Icing

Chocolate-Pecan Icing
½ cup butter or margarine
4 tablespoons cocoa
6 tablespoons milk
1 (16-ounce) package powdered
  sugar
1 teaspoon vanilla extract
1 cup chopped pecans

- Sift together first 4 ingredients in a large bowl.
- Bring 1 cup water and next 3 ingredients to a boil in a saucepan; pour over flour mixture, stirring well. Whisk together buttermilk, eggs, and vanilla; stir into chocolate batter. Pour batter into a greased and floured 9 x 13 x 2-inch pan.
- Bake at 400° for 20 minutes. Spread warm Chocolate-Pecan Icing over hot cake.

- Bring first 3 ingredients to a boil in a saucepan over medium-high heat, stirring constantly and being careful not to scorch. Stir in powdered sugar, vanilla, and pecans.

Yield: 12 servings

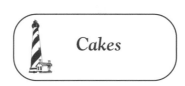

Mousse Cake

⅔ cup butter or margarine
1 cup whipping cream
1½ cups sugar, divided
1 cup cocoa
6 large eggs
1 teaspoon vanilla extract
¼ teaspoon salt
½ cup self-rising flour

- Preheat oven to 325°.
- Cook butter, cream, and ¾ cup sugar in a saucepan over low heat, stirring until melted. Remove from heat, and stir in cocoa. Freeze, stirring occasionally, 15 to 20 minutes or until slightly thickened.
- Beat eggs, vanilla, and salt at low speed with an electric mixer until blended; add remaining ¾ cup sugar and flour, beating at high speed 5 minutes or until light and fluffy. Stir one-fourth of egg mixture into cooled chocolate mixture; fold chocolate mixture into remaining egg mixture. Pour batter into a greased 9-inch springform pan.
- Bake at 325° for 55 to 60 minutes or until center is firm. Run a knife around edges to loosen from sides of pan; let cool on a wire rack. (Cake will fall in center.) Remove sides of pan, and spread with White Chocolate Glaze. Chill until glaze is firm.

White Chocolate Glaze
2 (6-ounce) packages white
    chocolate baking squares
¼ cup shortening
⅓ cup powdered sugar

- Cook all ingredients in a small saucepan over low heat, stirring constantly, until melted.

Yield: 1 (9-inch) cake

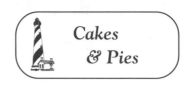

Mickie's Chocolate Cake

1 cup buttermilk
1 cup vegetable oil
1 teaspoon vanilla extract
1 large egg
2 cups sugar
2 cups all-purpose flour
1 tablespoon baking soda
½ teaspoon salt
½ cup cocoa
1 cup boiling water

- Beat first 4 ingredients at medium speed with an electric mixer until creamy; add sugar and next 4 ingredients, beating well. Add 1 cup boiling water, beating well (batter will be very soupy). Pour into a greased and floured 9 x 13 x 2-inch pan.
- Bake at 325° for 45 minutes or until done.

Yield: 10 servings

Foolproof Pie Crust

4 cups all-purpose flour
2½ teaspoons sugar
2 teaspoons salt
1¾ cups shortening
1 tablespoon vinegar
1 large egg
½ cup water

- Combine first 3 ingredients in a bowl; cut in shortening using a fork or a pastry blender until crumbly.
- Whisk together vinegar, egg, and ½ cup water in a separate bowl; add to flour mixture, stirring with a fork until dry ingredients are moistened. Mold dough into a ball. Chill at least 15 minutes, or up to 3 days. This dough may also be frozen. Roll portions of dough out on a lightly floured surface as needed.

Yield: 2 (9-inch) double crusts and 1 (9-inch) shell

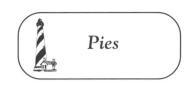

Mema's Buttermilk Custard Pie

1½ cups sugar

3 large eggs

¼ cup buttermilk

1 teaspoon vanilla extract

½ cup butter or margarine, melted

1 tablespoon all-purpose flour

1 unbaked 9-inch pastry shell

- Beat sugar and eggs at medium speed with an electric mixer until creamy; add buttermilk and next 3 ingredients, beating well. Pour into pastry shell.
- Bake at 350° for 40 to 50 minutes or until golden brown (check after 30 minutes; do not overcook).

Yield: 8 servings

Chocolate Pecan Pie

1 cup sugar

1 tablespoon cornstarch

1 tablespoon all-purpose flour

2 tablespoons cocoa

1 pinch of salt

2 large eggs

3 tablespoons butter or margarine, melted

⅔ cup milk

¾ cup flaked coconut

½ cup chopped pecans

1 teaspoon vanilla extract

1 unbaked 9-inch pastry shell

- Preheat oven to 400°.
- Stir together first 5 ingredients in a bowl; add eggs, butter, and milk, stirring well. Add coconut, pecans, and vanilla, stirring well. Pour into pastry shell.
- Bake at 400° for 35 to 40 minutes or until top is crusty and firm.

Yield: 8 servings

Scott's Fresh Apple Pie

Pastry for 1 (9-inch) 2-crust pie

¾ cup sugar

¼ cup all-purpose flour

½ teaspoon ground nutmeg

½ teaspoon ground cinnamon

Dash of salt

6 cups thinly sliced tart apple
(about 6 or 7 medium apples)

2 tablespoons butter or
margarine, cut up

- Preheat oven to 425°.
- Fit 1 prepared pie crust into a 9-inch pie plate. Combine sugar and next 4 ingredients in a large bowl; stir in apple slices. Spoon into prepared pie crust, and dot with butter.
- Top with remaining prepared pie crust. Seal and crimp edges. Cut slits in top of crust.
- Bake at 425° for 40 to 50 minutes or until crust is browned and juice bubbles through slits.

Yield: 6 to 8 servings

Peanut Butter Pie

1½ cups powdered sugar

1 cup creamy peanut butter

1 (8-ounce) package cream
cheese, softened

½ teaspoon vanilla extract

3 cups whipped cream or frozen
whipped topping, thawed

1 (6-ounce) chocolate crumb
crust

Garnishes: grated chocolate,
chopped peanuts

- Beat first 4 ingredients at medium speed with an electric mixer until smooth. Fold in 2 cups whipped cream, 1 cup at a time. Spoon into pie crust, smoothing top. Spread with remaining 1 cup whipped cream, and garnish, if desired. Freeze at least 3 hours and up to 2 weeks. Let stand at room temperature 20 minutes before serving.

Yield: 8 servings

Blueberry Pie

4 cups fresh blueberries, divided
¾ cup water
1 tablespoon butter or margarine
1 cup sugar
5 tablespoons cornstarch
⅛ teaspoon salt
⅛ teaspoon ground cinnamon
1 teaspoon lemon juice
1 baked 9-inch pastry shell
1 cup heavy cream, whipped

- Bring 1 cup blueberries and ¾ cup water to a boil in a saucepan; reduce heat, and simmer 4 minutes. Remove from heat, and stir in butter. Combine sugar and next 3 ingredients in a bowl; add to hot berry mixture, and cook over low heat, stirring often, until thickened. Remove from heat, and stir in lemon juice. Stir in remaining 3 cups berries. Pour into pastry shell. Chill until set.
- When ready to serve, spoon whipped cream into a pastry bag fitted with a tip; pipe a whipped cream border around edge of pie.

Yield: 6 to 8 servings

Lighthouse Lemon-Lime Pie

1 cup all-purpose flour
¼ cup firmly packed brown sugar
¾ cup chopped nuts
½ cup butter or margarine, melted
1 (14-ounce) can sweetened condensed milk
1 teaspoon grated lemon and lime rind
⅓ cup fresh lemon and lime juice

- Combine first 4 ingredients in a pan, stirring well.
- Bake at 350° for 20 minutes, stirring several times. Let cool. Spread mixture evenly in a pie plate. Combine sweetened condensed milk, lemon-lime rind, and juice, stirring well. Pour over crust. Chill until set.

Yield: 8 servings

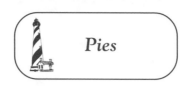

Flem Flams Fabulous Key Lime Pie

9 graham crackers

¼ cup sugar

⅓ cup butter, softened

4 egg yolks

1 (14-ounce) can sweetened condensed milk

½ cup fresh Key lime juice

1 teaspoon cream of tartar

- Preheat oven to 350°.
- Combine first 3 ingredients, stirring well. Press into a 9-inch pie plate.
- Bake at 350° for 8 minutes.
- Reduce oven temperature to 325°.
- Beat egg yolks at medium speed with an electric mixer until thick and pale; add sweetened condensed milk, beating well. Add half of lime juice, beating well. Add cream of tartar and remaining half of lime juice, beating well. Pour into prepared crust.
- Bake at 325° for 10 to 15 minutes or until center is firm. Let cool; freeze until set. Serve frozen.

Yield: 8 servings

Strawberry Pie

1 quart strawberries

1 cup sugar

¼ cup cornstarch

1 pinch of salt

½ cup water

1 baked 9-inch pastry shell

6 ounces whipped cream

- Mash half of strawberries in a saucepan; add sugar and next 3 ingredients, and cook over medium heat, stirring occasionally, until mixture is translucent. Let cool. Fold in remaining strawberries. Pour into pastry shell, and chill until set.
- Decorate pie with whipped cream as desired.

Yield: 8 servings

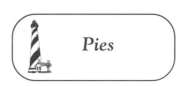
Grandma Rake's Florida Orange Meringue Pie

1⅓ cups sugar

7 tablespoons cornstarch

¼ teaspoon salt

1½ cups hot water

3 egg yolks, lightly beaten

½ cup fresh St. Augustine Wild Orange juice

2 tablespoons butter or margarine

1 baked 9-inch pastry shell

Meringue

- Preheat oven to 350°.
- Combine first 3 ingredients in a saucepan; gradually stir in 1½ cups hot water. Bring to a boil; reduce heat to medium, and cook, stirring constantly, 8 to 10 minutes or until thick and clear. Remove from heat.
- Combine several spoonfuls hot mixture and egg yolks in a bowl, stirring well; add to remaining hot mixture. Bring to a boil; reduce heat, and cook, stirring constantly, 4 to 5 minutes. Remove from heat, and gradually stir in orange juice and butter. Let cool. Pour pie filling into pastry shell; top with Meringue.
- Bake at 350° for 15 to 20 minutes or until lightly browned.

Meringue

3 egg whites

1 tablespoon orange juice

6 tablespoons sugar

- Beat egg whites and orange juice at medium speed with an electric mixer until soft peaks form. Gradually add sugar, beating until stiff peaks form.

Yield: 6 servings

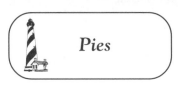

Daiquiri Pie

⅔ cup sugar

½ teaspoon salt

1 envelope unflavored gelatin

3 egg yolks, lightly beaten

½ cup fresh lime juice

¼ cup water

1 teaspoon grated lime rind

4 drops green liquid food coloring

¼ cup light rum

3 egg whites

⅓ cup sugar

1 baked 9-inch pastry shell

Garnishes: whipped cream, lime slices

- Combine first 3 ingredients in a saucepan; stir in yolks, lime juice, and ¼ cup water. Bring to a boil over medium heat, stirring constantly until gelatin dissolves. Remove from heat; stir in lime rind, food coloring, and rum. Chill until mixture begins to thicken.
- Beat egg whites at medium speed with an electric mixer until soft peaks form; gradually add sugar, beating until stiff peaks form. Fold in gelatin mixture. Chill until mixture mounds. Spoon into pastry shell; chill until firm. Garnish, if desired.

Yield: 8 servings

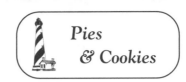
Chocolate Delight Pie

1 (12-ounce) package semisweet chocolate morsels, divided

½ cup skim milk

1 (8-ounce) package light cream cheese, softened

2 tablespoons sugar

1 (8-ounce) container light frozen whipped topping, thawed

1 (6-ounce) chocolate crumb crust

- Cook 1½ cups chocolate morsels and ¼ cup milk in a heavy saucepan over low heat, stirring constantly, until melted. Add remaining ¼ cup milk, cream cheese, and sugar, beating with a hand held mixer until smooth. Add whipped topping, stirring until smooth. Spoon into pie crust. Freeze 4 hours or until firm. Let stand at room temperature 30 minutes before serving.
- Melt remaining chocolate morsels in a heavy saucepan over low heat, stirring constantly. Drizzle over pie.

Yield: 8 servings

Banana-Oatmeal Cookies

1½ cups sifted all-purpose flour

½ teaspoon baking soda

1 teaspoon salt

1 cup sugar

¼ teaspoon ground nutmeg

¾ teaspoon ground cinnamon

¾ cup shortening

1 large egg, lightly beaten

1 cup mashed ripe banana (2 to 3 bananas)

1¾ cups quick-cooking rolled oats

¾ cup chopped nuts

- Sift together first 6 ingredients; cut in shortening using a pastry blender until mixture is crumbly. Add egg and next 3 ingredients, and beat at medium speed with an electric mixer until well blended. Drop dough by teaspoonfuls 1½ inches apart on greased cookie sheets.
- Bake at 400° for 15 minutes or until done.

Yield: 40 to 48 cookies

Meringue Cookies

½ cup sugar
¼ cup water
2 egg whites
1 pinch of cream of tartar
1 pinch of salt
Cocoa

- Bring sugar and ¼ cup water to a boil in a heavy saucepan over low heat; cover and boil over medium-high heat 5 minutes. Boil until a candy thermometer registers 250° (hard ball stage), washing down sugar crystals on sides of pan once with a brush dipped in cold water.
- Beat egg whites at low speed with an electric mixer until foamy; add cream of tartar and salt, and beat at medium-high speed until stiff peaks form. With mixer beating at medium speed, gradually add hot syrup. Beat 10 minutes or until stiff and cool.
- Spoon meringue into a pastry bag fitted with a #1A round metal tip. Pipe 25 quarter-size rounds onto a parchment paper-lined baking sheet. Dip your finger in cold water, and lightly smooth tops. Dust with cocoa.
- Bake at lowest oven temperature for 2 to 2½ hours or until dry. Store in an airtight container.

Yield: 25 cookies

Applesauce Cookies

2 cups all-purpose flour
1½ cups whole wheat flour
2 teaspoons baking soda
1 teaspoon salt
2 teaspoons ground cinnamon
1 teaspoon ground nutmeg
1 teaspoon ground cloves
2 cups sugar
1 cup shortening
2 large eggs, lightly beaten
2 cups applesauce
2 cups wheat bran cereal
2 cups raisins

- Sift together first 7 ingredients in a large bowl.
- Beat sugar and shortening at medium speed with a hand held mixer until creamy; add eggs and applesauce, stir well.
- Add bran and shortening mixture to flour mixture, and beat at medium speed with an electric mixer until blended. Add raisins, beating well. Drop dough by spoonfuls onto greased cookie sheets.
- Bake at 350° for 15 minutes or until browned.

Yield: 5 to 6 dozen

Russian Tea Cakes

1 cup butter or margarine, softened
½ cup sifted powdered sugar
1 teaspoon vanilla extract
2¼ cups all-purpose flour
¼ teaspoon salt
¾ cup finely chopped pecans
Powdered sugar

- Beat first 3 ingredients at medium speed with an electric mixer until creamy. Combine flour, salt, and pecans; gradually add to creamed mixture, beating well after each addition. Chill dough.
- Shape dough into 1-inch balls, and place on ungreased cookie sheets.
- Bake at 400° for 12 to 15 minutes or until edges are lightly browned. Roll warm cookies in powdered sugar. Let cool. Roll cookies in powdered sugar again.

Yield: 4 dozen

Nanimo Bars

1 cup butter or margarine,
  softened

10 tablespoons cocoa

2 large eggs

½ cup sugar

2 teaspoons vanilla extract

4 cups graham cracker crumbs

2 cups flaked coconut

1 cup chopped walnuts

3 tablespoons milk

1 envelope Birds vanilla custard
  mix

¼ cup butter or margarine,
  softened

Sifted powdered sugar
  (about ½ box)

8 (1-ounce) semisweet chocolate
  squares

2 tablespoons butter or margarine

- Combine first 5 ingredients in a
  bowl; set bowl in a larger bowl of
  boiling water. Stir mixture with
  a wooden spoon until butter is
  melted and mixture is custard
  consistency.
- Combine graham cracker
  crumbs, coconut, and nuts in a
  separate bowl; add to cocoa
  mixture, stirring well with
  wooden spoon. Press evenly and
  firmly into a 9 x 13 x 2-inch pan.
- Whisk together milk and custard
  mix; add ¼ cup butter, and beat
  at medium speed with an electric
  mixer until creamy. Beat in
  enough powdered sugar to reach
  frosting consistency. Spread over
  bottom layer.
- Microwave chocolate squares
  and 2 tablespoons butter at
  HIGH, stirring often, for
  10-second intervals until
  chocolate is melted. Spread over
  custard layer. Chill until set.
- Cut into squares, and store in
  the refrigerator.

Yield: 1 to 2 dozen

Gooey Butter Bars

½ cup butter or margarine,
   softened
1 (18.25-ounce) package yellow
   cake mix
1 large egg
¾ cup flaked coconut
½ cup finely chopped walnuts or
   pecans
1 (8-ounce) package cream
   cheese, softened
1 (16-ounce) package powdered
   sugar
1 teaspoon vanilla extract
2 large eggs

- Beat first 3 ingredients at medium speed with an electric mixer until a dough forms; stir in coconut and nuts (dough will be stiff). Press evenly into a greased 9 x 13 x 2-inch pan.
- Beat cream cheese and next 3 ingredients at medium speed with an electric mixer 5 minutes. Pour over prepared crust.
- Bake at 350° for 40 to 45 minutes or until topping is set. Let cool. Slice into squares.

Yield: 3 to 4 dozen

To press crust into pan, use greased wax paper so the dough doesn't stick to your hands.

Shortbread

¾ cup butter, softened
¼ cup sugar
2 cups all-purpose flour

- Beat butter and sugar at medium speed with an electric mixer until creamy; add flour, mixing well (if dough is crumbly beat in 1 to 2 more tablespoons butter). Roll dough to ½-inch thickness on a lightly floured surface. Cut into small shapes, and place ½ inch apart on ungreased cookie sheets.
- Bake at 350° for 20 minutes or until set. Immediately remove to wire racks to cool.

Yield: 1 to 2 dozen

Fruitcake Cookies

1 (8-ounce) package candied
   pineapple, chopped

1 (8-ounce) package candied
   cherries, chopped

1 (8-ounce) package dates,
   chopped

½ package golden raisins

3½ cups chopped pecans

3 cups sifted all-purpose flour,
   divided

1 cup butter or margarine

1 cup firmly packed light brown
   sugar

3 large eggs

½ teaspoon baking soda

1 teaspoon ground cinnamon

½ cup milk

½ teaspoon vanilla extract

- Preheat oven to 325°.
- Toss together first 5 ingredients
  and ½ cup flour to coat.
- Beat butter and sugar at medium
  speed with an electric mixer
  until creamy; add eggs, 1 at a
  time, beating well after each
  addition. Combine remaining
  2½ cups flour, soda, and
  cinnamon; add to creamed
  mixture alternately with milk
  and vanilla, beginning and
  ending with flour mixture and
  beating well after each addition.
  Stir in fruit and nuts. Drop
  dough by teaspoonfuls onto
  lightly greased cookie sheets.
- Bake at 325° for 15 minutes or
  until browned.

Yield: at least 3 dozen

Snickerdoodles

1 cup shortening

1½ cups sugar

2 large eggs

2¾ cups all-purpose flour

1 teaspoon baking soda

½ teaspoon salt

2 teaspoons cream of tartar

2 teaspoons ground cinnamon

3 tablespoons sugar

- Beat shortening and 1½ cups sugar at medium speed with an electric mixer until creamy; add eggs, beating well. Combine flour and next 3 ingredients; gradually add to creamed mixture, beating well after each addition. Chill dough.
- Combine cinnamon and 3 tablespoons sugar in a shallow dish. Shape dough into walnut-size balls, and roll in sugar mixture. Place 2 inches apart on ungreased cookie sheets.
- Bake at 375° for 12 minutes or until lightly browned. (Cookies will puff up at first, then flatten out with crinkled tops.)

Yield: 5 dozen

English Matrimonials

1½ cups all-purpose flour

1 cup firmly packed brown sugar

1½ cups regular rolled oats

¾ cup butter or margarine, softened

1 cup jam

- Combine first 3 ingredients; add butter, mixing well. Press two-thirds of mixture into a 9-inch square pan. Spread jam over bottom layer. Sprinkle remaining oat mixture over jam, pressing gently.
- Bake at 325° for 40 minutes. Let cool, and cut into squares.

Yield: 2 dozen

These are really good with strawberry or raspberry jam.

215

Pumpkin Cookies

1 cup butter or margarine
1 cup sugar
1 cup canned pumpkin
1 large egg
1 teaspoon vanilla extract
2 cups all-purpose flour
1 teaspoon baking powder
1 teaspoon baking soda
1 teaspoon ground cinnamon
½ teaspoon salt
½ cup chopped dates or raisins
½ cup chopped nuts

- Beat first 5 ingredients at medium speed with an electric mixer until creamy. Sift together flour and next 4 ingredients; add to creamed mixture, beating well. Stir in dates and nuts. Roll dough into 1-inch balls, and place on cookie sheets.
- Bake at 375° for 10 minutes.

Yield: 3 dozen

Pecan Tassies

½ cup butter or margarine, cut up
1 (3-ounce) package cream cheese
1 cup all-purpose flour
1½ cups firmly packed brown sugar
2 large eggs
1 teaspoon butter or margarine
1 cup chopped pecans

- Cut butter and cream cheese into flour using a pastry blender until crumbly. Shape dough into small balls, and press into miniature muffin pan cups.
- Combine sugar, eggs, and 1 teaspoon butter or margarine in a bowl. Spoon ½ teaspoon nuts in the bottom of each crust; top each with 1 teaspoon filling. Sprinkle each with ½ teaspoon nuts.
- Bake at 350° for 30 minutes.

Yield: 4 dozen

These tassies resemble small pecan pies.

216

Lemon Squares

2 cups all-purpose flour
½ cup powdered sugar
1 pinch of salt
1 cup butter or margarine, cut up
4 large eggs, lightly beaten
2 cups granulated sugar
6 tablespoons all-purpose flour
1 tablespoon grated lemon rind
6 tablespoons fresh lemon juice
Powdered sugar

- Combine first 3 ingredients; cut in butter with a pastry blender until crumbly. Press evenly into a 9 x 13 x 2-inch baking dish coated with vegetable cooking spray.
- Bake at 350° for 20 minutes.
- Beat eggs and next 4 ingredients at medium speed with an electric mixer until smooth; spread over prepared crust.
- Bake at 350° for 25 minutes. Let cool. Sift powdered sugar over top, and cut into squares.

Yield: 3 to 4 dozen

These freeze well. Wait until thawed and ready to serve before sprinkling with powdered sugar.

Chocolate-Peanut Butter Balls (Ohio Buckeye Candy)

3 cups creamy peanut butter
¾ cup butter or margarine, softened
2 (16-ounce) packages powdered sugar
2 (8-ounce) packages unsweetened chocolate squares

- Combine first 3 ingredients; shape mixture into small balls.
- Melt chocolate squares according to package directions. Dip peanut butter balls into melted chocolate until almost covered, using wooden picks and leaving a small portion of peanut butter mixture exposed at the top. Chill until ready to serve.

Yield: 3 dozen

Pecan Pie Cookies

1 cup butter or margarine, melted

2 cups all-purpose flour

1 cup firmly packed light brown
sugar

4 large eggs, lightly beaten

¼ cup all-purpose flour

3 cups firmly packed dark brown
sugar

1 (3-ounce) can coconut,
shredded

2 cups pecans, chopped

1 teaspoon salt

½ teaspoon vanilla extract

Powdered sugar

- Preheat oven to 350°.
- Combine first 3 ingredients;
  press evenly into a 9 x 13 x 2-
  inch pan.
- Bake at 350° for 15 minutes. Let
  cool.
- Reduce oven temperature to
  325°.
- Combine eggs and next 6
  ingredients; spread over prepared
  crust.
- Bake at 325° for 40 minutes or
  until mixture is firm. Remove
  from oven, and sprinkle with
  powdered sugar. Let cool and cut
  into squares.

4 dozen

These rich, delicious cookies will keep in the freezer several months.

Chocolate Chip Cookies

½ cup butter, softened
½ cup margarine, softened
¾ cup granulated sugar
¾ cup firmly packed brown sugar
1 teaspoon vanilla extract
2 large eggs
2¼ cups all-purpose flour
1 teaspoon baking soda
1 teaspoon salt
½ cup semisweet chocolate
    morsels
½ cup butterscotch morsels
¼ cup chopped nuts
¼ cup flaked coconut

• Beat butter and margarine at medium speed with an electric mixer until creamy; add sugars, beating well. Add vanilla and eggs, beating well. Combine flour, soda, and salt; add to creamed mixture, beating well. Stir in chocolate morsels and next 3 ingredients. Drop dough by spoonfuls onto lightly greased cookie sheets.
• Bake at 375° for 10 minutes.

Yield: 3 dozen

Cinnamon Crispies

¾ cup butter or margarine
1 cup sugar
2 to 2¼ teaspoons ground
    cinnamon
1 teaspoon vanilla extract
1 large egg, separated
2 cups sifted all-purpose flour
¼ teaspoon salt
½ cup chopped pecans (optional)

• Beat first 3 ingredients at medium speed with an electric mixer until creamy; add vanilla and egg yolk, beating well. Add flour and salt, beating well. Spread into a greased 10 x 15-inch jelly-roll pan, covering dough with wax paper and spreading with a rolling pin. Remove wax paper, and brush with egg white; sprinkle with nuts, if desired.
• Bake at 325° for 35 minutes. Remove from oven, and immediately cut into diamond shapes.

Yield: at least 2 dozen

Cherry Oat Crunchies

1 cup unsalted butter, softened
¾ cup firmly packed light brown
   sugar
1 large egg
1 teaspoon vanilla extract
1½ cups all-purpose flour
1 teaspoon baking soda
1 cup dried cherries
1 cup miniature chocolate
   morsels
1 cup English toffee candy bar
   pieces
1 cup regular rolled oats

- Beat butter at medium speed with an electric mixer until creamy; add sugar, and beat until light and fluffy. Add egg and vanilla, beating well. Sift together flour and soda. Stir flour mixture, cherries, and next 3 ingredients into dough. Divide dough into thirds, and shape each portion into a log. Wrap in plastic wrap, and chill.
- Cut dough into ½- to ¾-inch-thick slices, and place on parchment paper-lined cookie sheets.
- Bake at 350° for 8 to 10 minutes.

Yield: 3 dozen

Oatmeal-Molasses Cookies

4 cups regular rolled oats
1¼ cups sugar
½ tablespoon ground ginger
4 cups sifted all-purpose flour
1 tablespoon baking soda
½ teaspoon salt
2 large eggs, lightly beaten
⅓ cup hot water
1½ cups seedless raisins
1 cup finely chopped walnuts
1 cup melted shortening
1 cup molasses
Sugar

- Combine first 3 ingredients in a large bowl. Sift together flour, soda, and salt in a separate bowl. Add flour mixture, eggs, and next 5 ingredients to oat mixture, and beat at medium speed with an electric mixer until well blended. Roll dough to ¼-inch thickness on a lightly floured surface. Cut cookies with a 3-inch round cookie cutter, and place 1½ to 2 inches apart on a well-greased cookie sheet. Brush cookies with water, and sprinkle with sugar.
- Bake at 375° for 8 to 10 minutes.

Yield: 5 to 6 dozen

Almond Butter Cookies

1 cup unsalted butter, softened
1 cup sugar
¼ teaspoon almond extract
1 large egg
1 (8-ounce) can almond paste
1½ cups sifted all-purpose flour
½ teaspoon baking powder
¼ teaspoon baking soda
¼ teaspoon salt
Sugar
Sliced almonds

- Beat first 3 ingredients at medium speed with an electric mixer until light and fluffy. Add egg and almond paste, beating well. Sift together flour and next 3 ingredients; add to creamed mixture, beating well. Chill dough at least 2 hours or until thoroughly chilled.
- Preheat oven to 350°.
- Roll dough, 2 teaspoonfuls at a time, into balls. Roll balls in sugar, and place on ungreased cookie sheets. Flatten cookies slightly with the flat bottom of a glass that has been dipped in sugar. Press a few almond slices into the top of each cookie.
- Bake at 350° for 8 to 10 minutes. Transfer cookies to a wire rack, and let cool. Store in an airtight container.

Yield: 2 to 3 dozen

Blueberry Sauce

¾ cup water
¼ cup sugar
1 tablespoon lemon juice
1 teaspoon cornstarch
1 tablespoon water
1 cup fresh or frozen blueberries

- Bring ¾ cup water and sugar to a boil in a small saucepan, stirring until sugar dissolves. Stir in lemon juice. Combine cornstarch and 1 tablespoon water; add to saucepan, and cook 1 minute. Stir in blueberries, and cook 30 seconds.

221

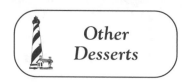

Awesome Fudge

4½ cups sugar
1 can evaporated milk
1½ teaspoons vanilla extract
2 (12-ounce) packages semisweet
    chocolate morsels
1 (15-ounce) sweet chocolate bar
1 (7-ounce) jar marshmallow
    cream

- Bring sugar and milk to a boil in a saucepan; boil 5 minutes.
- Combine vanilla and next 3 ingredients in the top of a large double boiler; bring water to a boil, and cook, stirring constantly, until chocolate is melted. Add milk mixture to chocolate mixture, stirring well. Pour into a well-buttered 9 x 13 x 2-inch pan. Let cool. Cut into small squares.

Yield: 6 dozen pieces

Truffles

2 (8-ounce) packages semisweet
    chocolate squares, chopped
1½ cups whipping cream
Cocoa
Finely chopped nuts (optional)

- Combine chocolate and cream in the top of a double boiler; bring water to a boil, and cook over medium-low heat, stirring constantly, until chocolate is melted. Chill until firm.
- Dust palms with cocoa, and roll chocolate mixture into balls. Roll balls in nuts, if desired. Chill or freeze until ready to serve.

Yield: 2½ dozen

These are soooo good! Keep the chocolate mixture well chilled. It becomes sticky if it sits out too long and gets hard to roll.

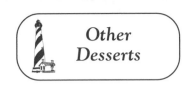
Really Good Brownies

1½ cups butter

1 (8-ounce) package
  unsweetened chocolate

6 large eggs

3 cups sugar

1½ cups all-purpose flour

3 teaspoons vanilla extract

1 cup chopped walnuts or pecans
  (optional)

- Preheat oven to 350°.
- Combine butter and chocolate in the top of a double boiler; bring water to a boil, and cook over low heat, stirring often, until melted. Remove from heat, and stir well.
- Beat eggs at medium speed with an electric mixer; gradually beat in sugar. Add chocolate mixture, beating well. Stir in flour, vanilla, and, if desired, nuts (do not over mix). Pour batter into 2 buttered 9-inch square pans.
- Bake at 350° for 20 to 25 minutes or until a wooden pick inserted in center comes out with moist crumbs (do not over bake; center should be moist). Let cool, and cut into squares.

You may substitute 1½ cups cocoa mixed with ½ cup vegetable oil for chocolate, if desired. Do not try to bake these brownies in a 9 x 13 x 2-inch baking dish; the edges will burn before the center is done.

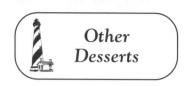

Flan

¾ cup sugar
4 large eggs
1 (14-ounce) can sweetened
  condensed milk
1 cup water
1 teaspoon vanilla extract
Garnish: fresh berries

• Preheat oven to 350°.
• Cook sugar in a heavy skillet over low heat, stirring constantly with a wooden spoon, until golden. Pour into a 1-quart baking dish, spreading with spoon to coat bottom and sides evenly. Let cool.
• Beat eggs at medium speed with an electric mixer; add milk, 1 cup water, and vanilla, beating well. Pour into prepared baking dish.
• Bake in a 1-inch hot water bath at 350° for 1 hour or until a knife inserted ½ inch in center comes out clean. Let cool completely (about 2 hours).
• Run a spatula around edges of flan, and invert onto a serving dish. Pour caramel over flan. Chill. Garnish, if desired.

Yield: 6 to 8 servings

Mary Jane's Fudge Chews

2 cups sugar
½ cup milk
¼ cup butter or margarine
3 tablespoons cocoa
3 cups quick-cooking rolled oats
½ cup peanut butter
1 teaspoon vanilla extract

• Bring first 4 ingredients to a boil in a saucepan; boil 1 minute. Remove from heat, and stir in oats, peanut butter, and vanilla. Drop by teaspoonfuls onto wax paper. Let cool.

Yield: about 5 dozen

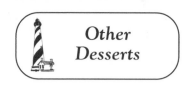
Rocky Road Squares

1 (12-ounce) package semisweet
  chocolate morsels
1 (14-ounce) can sweetened
  condensed milk
2 tablespoons butter or
  margarine
1 jar dry roasted peanuts
1 (10-ounce) package miniature
  marshmallows

- Place chocolate morsels in the top of a double boiler; bring water to a boil, and cook, stirring constantly, until melted. Add milk and butter, and cook, stirring often, until thickened.
- Combine peanuts and marshmallows in a large bowl; pour chocolate mixture over top, stirring well. Pour fudge into a wax paper-lined 9 x 13 x 2-inch pan. Chill until set. Cut into squares.

Yield: 4 to 5 dozen

Apple Streusel

1½ cups sugar, divided
1 teaspoon ground cinnamon
6 to 8 cooking apples, peeled and
  thinly sliced
Butter or margarine, cut up
1 cup all-purpose flour
1 teaspoon baking powder
½ teaspoon salt
1 large egg

- Preheat oven to 350°.
- Combine ½ cup sugar and cinnamon. Layer apple slices in a buttered 9 x 13 x 2-inch baking dish; sprinkle with sugar mixture. Dot with butter.
- Sift together remaining 1 cup sugar, flour, baking powder, and salt; add egg, stirring until crumbly. Sprinkle evenly over apple slices.
- Bake at 350° for 35 to 45 minutes or until crust is browned. Serve with cream, whipped cream, or ice cream.

Yield: 8 to 12 servings

French Mint Bars

3 (1-ounce) unsweetened
  chocolate squares, divided
½ cup butter or margarine
2 large eggs
1 cup sugar
¼ teaspoon peppermint extract
½ cup all-purpose flour
½ cup walnuts
½ teaspoon salt
2 tablespoons butter or margarine

- Combine 2 chocolate squares and ½ cup butter in the top of a double boiler; bring water to a boil, and cook, stirring constantly, until melted. Let cool. Add eggs to chocolate mixture, beating with a hand held mixer until smooth. Add sugar and next 4 ingredients, beating well. Pour into a greased 8-inch square pan.
- Bake at 350° for 18 to 22 minutes. Let cool.
- Microwave remaining 1 chocolate square and 2 tablespoons butter at HIGH, stirring often, for 10-second intervals until melted.
- Spread Peppermint Frosting over brownies, and pour chocolate glaze over frosting.

Peppermint Frosting
2 tablespoons butter or margarine
1 cup powdered sugar
1 tablespoon milk
¾ teaspoon peppermint extract

- Beat butter and powdered sugar at medium speed with an electric mixer until creamy; add milk and peppermint extract, beating well.

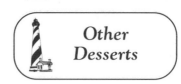

Bananas Griffith

¼ cup butter or margarine
1 egg yolk
1 teaspoon dry mustard
½ cup sugar
Juice of 1 lemon
3 to 4 firm, ripe bananas

- Melt butter in a skillet over low heat.
- Whisk together egg yolk, mustard, and sugar; gradually stir in lemon juice alternately with melted butter. Let cool.
- Slice bananas into a serving dish; pour dressing over top, stirring gently to coat.

This dish improves with some time to marinate, but does not store well overnight.

Cream Puffs in a Pan

1 cup water
½ cup butter or margarine
1 cup all-purpose flour
4 large eggs
1 (8-ounce) package cream cheese, softened
2 (3.4-ounce) packages vanilla instant pudding mix
4 cups milk
1 (12-ounce) container frozen whipped topping, thawed

- Bring 1 cup water and butter to a boil in a saucepan; add flour, stirring with a fork until mixture forms a dough mound. Transfer to a large bowl, and add eggs, 1 at a time, beating well after each addition. Spread onto a greased 10 x 15-inch jelly-roll pan.
- Bake at 400° for 25 to 30 minutes. Let cool.
- Beat cream cheese at medium speed with an electric mixer until creamy; add pudding mix, beating well. Add milk, beating until smooth and thickened. Spread over puff crust, and top with whipped topping. Cut into small squares, and serve immediately.

Yield: 3 to 4 dozen

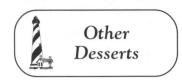

Cordial Cherries

12 maraschino cherries, drained
¼ cup brandy
4 (1-ounce) semisweet chocolate
   squares

- Combine cherries and brandy in a bowl; freeze. Remove frozen cherries from brandy, wiping with a paper towel.
- Microwave chocolate squares in a microwave-safe bowl at HIGH, stirring often, for 10-second intervals until melted. Quickly dip frozen cherries into melted chocolate, swirling until completely covered. Chill until ready to serve.

Yield: 1 dozen

Peach-Blueberry Cobbler

½ cup butter or margarine
1 cup all-purpose flour
1¼ cups sugar, divided
2 teaspoons baking powder
½ cup milk
2 cups sliced fresh peaches
2 cups fresh blueberries

- Melt butter in a 2½-quart baking dish in a 350° oven.
- Combine flour, ¾ cup sugar, and baking powder in a bowl; add milk, stirring until blended. Spoon batter over melted butter (do not stir).
- Combine remaining ½ cup sugar, peaches, and blueberries. Spoon over batter (do not stir).
- Bake at 350° for 45 to 55 minutes.

Yield: 8 servings

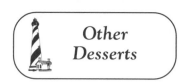

Cream Pralines

1 (16-ounce) package light
   brown sugar
¾ cup evaporated milk
⅛ teaspoon salt
1 tablespoon butter or margarine
2 cups pecan halves or pieces

• Cook first 4 ingredients in a saucepan over low heat, stirring constantly, until sugar dissolves. Add pecans, and cook over medium heat, stirring constantly, until a candy thermometer register 236° (soft ball stage). Remove from heat; let cool 5 minutes. Stir rapidly with a wooden spoon until mixture thickens and coats pecans. Drop spoonfuls rapidly onto aluminum foil or wax paper. (Stir in a few drops of hot water if candy gets too thick.) Let patties stand until set.

Yield: 3½ dozen

For a different flavor, stir 1 teaspoon vanilla extract, rum, or maple flavoring into candy after removing from heat.

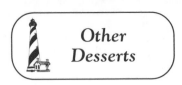
Praline Nuts

2½ cups pecan halves
1 cup sugar
½ cup water
1 teaspoon ground cinnamon
½ teaspoon salt
1½ teaspoons vanilla extract

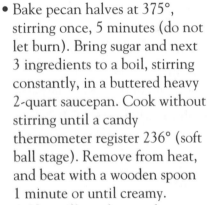

- Bake pecan halves at 375°, stirring once, 5 minutes (do not let burn). Bring sugar and next 3 ingredients to a boil, stirring constantly, in a buttered heavy 2-quart saucepan. Cook without stirring until a candy thermometer register 236° (soft ball stage). Remove from heat, and beat with a wooden spoon 1 minute or until creamy.
- Add vanilla and toasted pecan halves to sugar mixture, stirring gently until pecans are coated. Turn out onto a buttered platter or cookie sheet. Separate immediately, using 2 forks. Let stand until set. Store in an airtight container.

Yield: 1 pound

This & That

The Oldest House

In the early decades of the twentieth century there were three competing "Oldest" houses in St. Augustine. This persisted until the St. Augustine Historical Society acquired all three, closed down two, and settled upon the two-story house at 14 St. Francis Street as the only one to bear the title.

Through its centuries the house has grown outward and upward, then shrunk back as later additions were removed.

It is known to many as the setting for Eugenia Price's *Maria* (1977), one of a trilogy of popular Florida novels she wrote.

Among other distinctions, this was once the home of Miss Emma L. Grout who, at the age of 74 in 1920, became the first woman to register to vote in St. Augustine.

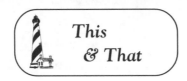

Easy Exchanges

Check the first three categories for cup, tablespoon or teaspoon equivalents of liquid or dry ingredients. For fluid-ounce equivalents, see the last category.

MEASURE	EQUALS
Teaspoons	
Under ⅛ teaspoon	Dash or pinch
1½ teaspoons	½ tablespoon
3 teaspoons	1 tablespoon
Tablespoons	
1 tablespoon	3 teaspoons
4 tablespoons	¼ cup
5⅓ tablespoons	⅓ cup
8 tablespoons	½ cup
10⅔ tablespoons	⅔ cup
16 tablespoons	1 cup
Cups	
¼ cup	4 tablespoons
⅓ cup	5⅓ tablespoons
½ cup	8 tablespoons
½ cup	¼ pint
⅔ cup	10⅔ tablespoons
1 cup	16 tablespoons
1 cup	½ pint
2 cups	1 pint
4 cups	1 quart
Liquid Measures	
2 tablespoons	1 fluid ounce
3 tablespoons	1 jigger
¼ cup	2 fluid ounces
½ cup	4 fluid ounces
1 cup	8 fluid ounces

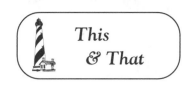

How to Know What You Need

Making a shopping list based on a recipe can be tricky if you don't know how many tomatoes yields 3 cups chopped. Our handy translations:

WHEN THE RECIPE CALLS FOR:	YOU NEED:
4 cups shredded cabbage	1 small cabbage
1 cup grated raw carrot	1 large carrot
2½ cups sliced carrots	1 pound raw carrots
4 cups cooked cut fresh green beans	1 pound beans
1 cup chopped onion	1 large onion
4 cups sliced raw potatoes	4 medium-size potatoes
1 cup chopped sweet pepper	1 large pepper
1 cup chopped tomato	1 large tomato
2 cups canned tomatoes	16-ounce can
4 cups sliced apples	4 medium-size apples
1 cup mashed banana	3 medium-size bananas
1 teaspoon grated lemon rind	1 medium-size lemon
2 tablespoons lemon juice	1 medium-size lemon
4 teaspoons grated orange rind	1 medium-size orange
1 cup orange juice	3 medium-size oranges
4 cups sliced peaches	8 medium-size peaches
2 cups sliced strawberries	1 pint
1 cup soft bread crumbs	2 slices fresh bread
1 cup bread cubes	2 slices fresh bread
2 cups shredded Swiss or Cheddar cheese	8 ounces cheese
1 cup egg whites	6 or 7 large eggs
1 egg white	2 teaspoons egg white powder + 2 tablespoons water
4 cups chopped walnuts or pecans	1 pound shelled

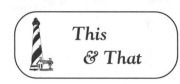

Ingredient Substitutions

INSTEAD OF:	AMOUNT:	USE:
Arrowroot	1 teaspoon	1 tablespoon flour
	2 teaspoons	1 tablespoon cornstarch
Bacon bits	1 tablespoon	1 slice bacon
Baking powder	1 teaspoon	¼ teaspoon baking soda + ½ teaspoon cream of tartar + ¼ teaspoon cornstarch
Baking powder, double-acting	1 teaspoon	1½ teaspoons phosphate baking powder or 2 teaspoons tartrate baking powder
Bay leaf, ground	⅛ teaspoon	1 whole bay leaf
Bay leaf, crumbled	¼ teaspoon	1 whole bay leaf
Beef soup base	1½ teaspoons	1 bouillon cube
	1 tablespoon + 1 cup water	1 cup beef stock
	1 teaspoon	1 teaspoon beef extract
Butter	1 cup	1 cup margarine or 1 cup shortening + butter flavoring, or ⅘ cup bacon drippings + ¼ cup liquid, or ⅞ cup vegetable oil
Buttermilk	1 cup	1 cup yogurt, or 1 cup warm milk + 1 tablespoon white vinegar or lemon juice; allow to stand for 10 minutes
Cake flour	1 cup	1 cup less 2 tablespoons white flour + 2 tablespoons cornstarch
Cardamom, ground	½ teaspoon	10 whole pods (pod removed, seeds crushed)

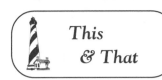

INSTEAD OF:	AMOUNT:	USE:
Chicken soup base	1½ teaspoons 1 tablespoon + 1 cup water	1 chicken bouillon cube 1 cup chicken stock
Chocolate, unsweetened	1 square	3 tablespoons cocoa + 2 teaspoons shortening
Chocolate, semisweet	1 square	3 tablespoons cocoa + 2 teaspoons shortening + 3 tablespoons sugar
Cornstarch	1 tablespoon	2 tablespoons white flour or 1 tablespoon arrowroot, or 1 tablespoon tapioca
Cracker crumbs	¾ cup	1 cup dry bread crumbs
Cream	1 cup	¾ cup milk plus ⅓ cup melted butter
Egg	1 egg	2 yolks for thickening
Flour, white	1 cup	1⅛ cups cake flour, or 1⅛ cups whole wheat flour, or 1⅓ cups rye flour
Garlic, minced	1 teaspoon	1 clove fresh garlic
Garlic powder	½ teaspoon	1 clove fresh garlic
Ginger, fresh chopped	1 teaspoon	2 teaspoons crystallized ginger (rinse off sugar coating) or ¼ teaspoon ground ginger
Herbs, dried	1 teaspoon	1 tablespoon fresh herb
Honey	1 cup	1 cup corn syrup, or 1¼ cups sugar + ¼ cup water
Horseradish, prepared	2 tablespoons	1 tablespoon dry horseradish + 1 tablespoon water
Lemon peel, dried	1 teaspoon	1 teaspoon fresh grated peel, or grated peel of 1 medium lemon, or ½ teaspoon lemon extract

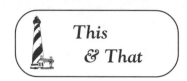

Measure for Measure

Quick: How much cooked white rice does one raw cup yield? Answer: Three cups. We unravel this and other mysteries cooks face time and again.

AMOUNT	MEASURE
Berries 1 pint	2¼ cups
Butter or Margarine ½ stick 1 pound	¼ cup or 4 tablespoons 4 sticks or 2 cups
Cheese 8 ounces cream cheese 8 ounces cottage cheese 4 ounces Parmesan, grated	1 cup 1 cup 1¼ cups
Chocolate 1 square 1 6-ounce package semisweet pieces	1 ounce 1 cup

Cookies
For 1 cup of crumbs:
  19 chocolate wafers
  22 vanilla wafers
  14 graham cracker squares	

Cream 1 cup heavy cream	2 cups whipped
Dried Beans and Peas 1 cup	2¼ cups cooked
Herbs 1 tablespoon fresh	1 teaspoon dried

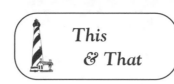

AMOUNT	MEASURE
Pasta	
8 ounces elbow macaroni	4 cups cooked
8 ounces medium-wide noodles	3¾ cups cooked
8 ounces fine noodles	5½ cups cooked
8 ounces spaghetti	4 cups cooked
Rice	
1 cup white	3 cups cooked
1 cup converted	4 cups cooked
1 cup instant	1½ cups cooked
1 cup brown	3 to 4 cups cooked
Sugar	
1 pound granulated	2 cups
1 pound brown, firmly packed	2¼ cups
1 pound confectioners'	4½ cups

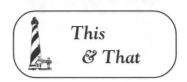

Approximate Metric Equivalents

¼ teaspoon	=	1.23 milliliters
½ teaspoon	=	2.46 milliliters
¾ teaspoon	=	3.7 milliliters
1 teaspoon	=	4.93 milliliters
1¼ teaspoons	=	6.16 milliliters
1½ teaspoons	=	7.39 milliliters
1¾ teaspoons	=	8.63 milliliters
2 teaspoons	=	9.86 milliliters
1 tablespoon	=	14.79 milliliters
2 tablespoons	=	29.57 milliliters
¼ cup	=	59.15 milliliters
½ cup	=	118.3 milliliters
1 cup	=	236.59 milliliters
2 cups or 1 pint	=	473.18 milliliters
3 cups	=	709.77 milliliters
4 cups or 1 quart	=	946.36 milliliters
4 quarts or 1 gallon	=	3.785 liters

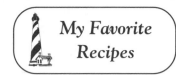

My Favorite Recipes

RECIPE:	PAGE NUMBER:

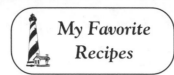

My Favorite Recipes

RECIPE:	PAGE NUMBER:

Index

Fountain of Youth

One of the oldest American legends is that Ponce de Leon discovered Florida while he was searching for the Fountain of Youth—unlike his conquistadorial colleagues who were merely searching for gold and silver.

This has led many Florida places to claim to be the miraculous site. St. Augustine has had two of them.

The first, Ponce de Leon Springs off Masters Drive in West Augustine, was promoted in the 1870s by real estate entrepreneur John Whitney, whose son later added an alligator farm to the property.

The second, and current, claimant was discovered in the early twentieth century by a colorful character named Luella Day McConnell, who came here after participating in the Yukon Gold Rush. A later owner was longtime St. Augustine Mayor Walter B. Fraser.

An array of famous people—including evangelist Billy Sunday and aviator Eddie Rickenbacker—have quaffed the water here.

Index

Index

Index

Index

Index

Index

Index

Index

Index

Index

Index

Index

Index

Lighthouse Secrets

Junior Service League of St. Augustine, Inc.
P.O. Box 374
St. Augustine, FL 32085

Please send ___ copy(ies) of *Lighthouse Secrets*   @ $19.95 each _____

             Postage and handling   @ $ 3.50 each _____

                                      Total _____

Name _____

Address _____

City _____ State _____ Zip _____

Make checks payable to Junior Service League of St. Augustine, Inc.

Lighthouse Secrets

Junior Service League of St. Augustine, Inc.
P.O. Box 374
St. Augustine, FL 32085

Please send ___ copy(ies) of *Lighthouse Secrets*   @ $19.95 each _____

             Postage and handling   @ $ 3.50 each _____

                                      Total _____

Name _____

Address _____

City _____ State _____ Zip _____

Make checks payable to Junior Service League of St. Augustine, Inc.